Preparing collections
for digitization

Preparing collections for digitization

Anna E. Bülow and Jess Ahmon

with contributions from Ross Spencer

facet publishing

In association with the National Archives

© Crown copyright 2011
Published by Facet Publishing
7 Ridgmount Street, London WC1E 7AE
www.facetpublishing.co.uk

Facet Publishing is wholly owned by CILIP: the Chartered Institute of Library and Information Professionals.

Anna E. Bülow and Jess Ahmon have asserted their right under the Copyright, Designs and Patents Act 1988 to be identified as authors of this work.

British Library Cataloguing in Publication Data
A catalogue record for this book is available from the British Library.

ISBN 978-1-85604-711-1

First published 2011
Reprinted digitally

Text printed on FSC accredited material.

Mixed Sources
Product group from well-managed
forests and other controlled sources
www.fsc.org Cert no. SA-COC-1565
© 1996 Forest Stewardship Council
FSC

Typeset from authors' files in 10/14 pt Palatino and Humanist 777 by Facet Publishing.
Printed and made in Great Britain by the MPG Books Group, UK.

Contents

Acknowledgements

The National Archives UK has been developing its digitization programme over many years. This has been a collaborative effort and we could not have achieved what we have without the work of many colleagues across the archive and beyond, past and present.

The authors would like to thank the following people in particular for their support in writing this book: Tanja de Boer (National Library of the Netherlands), Liam Greenshields (Imaging Department, Imperial College Healthcare NHS Trust) and Jonas Palm (National Archives of Sweden). We would also like to thank Alan Stitt for reviewing the manuscript, as well as our colleagues from The National Archives UK: Nancy Bell, Caroline Kimbell and Laura Simpson.

List of figures and tables

Figures

Tables

Introduction

Digitization is a complex business involving not only image capture, transcription, indexing and delivery but also technical issues around online presentation, digital file management and digital preservation. At the same time, digitization projects are high-risk ventures where successful implementation is critical. While much has been written on the various elements of digitization, the practical aspects have often been neglected. These practical details are significant not only in safeguarding the collection during image capture but also in ensuring that image capture runs smoothly and successfully.

Preparing Collections for Digitization aims to address this perceived gap in the literature by focusing on the actual image capture operation with particular emphasis on all matters concerning the preservation and preparation of the original documents. It is intended that this book should complement rather than replace existing publications. Wider issues such as metadata capture, delivery systems and project management in general are equally significant but since they are covered amply elsewhere they are not addressed here.

Since this book focuses on preservation issues it is aimed specifically at the person with responsibility for preservation of the collection, referred to in the text as the collection manager. In larger institutions this may be the head of the conservation department; in smaller institutions it could be a senior archivist or librarian, a curator or registrar. The collection manager is not necessarily a conservator and so professional jargon is avoided, but it is assumed that the reader is acquainted with basic principles of preservation such as the importance of good storage, housing and handling. There are some processes that should only be carried out by a trained conservator and these are clearly indicated in the text. While this book is of primary relevance to the collection manager it is hoped that it would also be of use to those who manage digitization projects as it provides a valuable insight into preservation concerns. Much of the guidance given here would also be useful for those in the information management industry who seek to work with heritage institutions on digitization projects.

The text largely draws on experiences at The National Archives UK, where the collection consists of a wide variety of materials, media and formats. However, many of the principles and processes described here can also be applied to digitization in a library context, or anywhere where hand-written or printed heritage is to be digitized in a systematic way. This book is particularly relevant for the digitization of collections of very diverse materials and where the documents are of varying condition, but it is valid for any collection for which long-term preservation is a priority.

The book begins by examining how digitization projects can aid the preservation of a collection if appropriately planned and executed, and how digital technology has prompted a shift in institutional focus. Chapter 2 'Before you digitize: resources, suppliers and surrogates' looks specifically at some of the strategic issues that need to be addressed at the outset. The resulting digital image is of pivotal importance and its size, quality and technical aspects have to be well considered before embarking on the project. Here, we have drawn on the experience of Ross Spencer (Technical Researcher in Digital Preservation at The National Archives UK) for Chapter 3 'The digital image'. His contribution to this publication is gratefully acknowledged.

The remaining chapters cover the end-to-end process of image capture from selecting collections for digitization to choosing equipment and preparing documents, as well as all the issues that will have a bearing on document preservation when setting up the image capture operation. Through their involvement with digitization projects, the collection manager can ensure the welfare of the collection throughout the digitization process. However, the collection manager also has a vital role to play in ensuring effective and efficient image capture. This section of the book serves as a 'how to' reference manual, informing the decision-making process and supporting those who may need to make difficult decisions.

Digitization will contribute to the preservation of a collection in the long term but requires a significant investment of resources. One of the key themes of this book is therefore the importance of planning in order to avoid costly mistakes.

It is hoped that this publication will assist those who are embarking on a digitization programme or those who are managing existing projects so as to safeguard documents, facilitate the digitization process and maximize the benefits in the long term.

Anna E. Bülow and Jess Ahmon

1

Digitization in the context of collection management

Introduction

Digitization projects take place within the context of a global market and institutional goals. The dramatic growth in digitization since the late 1990s is a direct response to the rapid development of the internet and corresponding changes in user expectations. This is part of an overall shift within the heritage sector as a whole and has had an inevitable impact on the way that collections are managed, and the role of the conservator.

The impact of new technologies

The internet has become the principle source of information on many aspects of life for millions of people of all generations. This digital revolution has fundamentally changed the way that we live and work. While there are great benefits to the availability of information via the internet, it has put new pressures on libraries, archives and museums. Increasingly, people expect to find and retrieve information online, especially the generation who have grown up with the internet and have often not learned to use and interrogate catalogues. Research using catalogue information typically leads to focused exploration of a subject in a particular context. In contrast, the internet works on a keyword search basis. Search results via keywords on the internet are vast, and the enormity of information thrown up often leads to an assumption that information not available on the internet is nonexistent. The growth of the internet has therefore fostered a new generation of users who not only expect all information to be available online but also expect it to be fully searchable.

At the same time, new technologies have brought new opportunities for cultural institutions – many libraries and archives have been involved with digitizing their collections for some years now. Digitizing collections has a great number of benefits, many of which go beyond the most obvious of increasing the general accessibility of a collection (Hughes, 2004, 9–16). Making a collection available online will facilitate access to it for a much broader audience. This can result in a shift from traditional users, such as academic researchers coming to use original material within an institution's reading room, to a much broader and more diverse user-base who will discover and subsequently use information that did not previously seem available to them.

Furthermore, digital technology can enhance access, allowing the user to browse and compare content and enabling an institution to link the content of its own collection with other relevant online material, thus building up a large pool of interlinked information. Digitization therefore offers the possibility to develop a collection through bridging the gaps within one's own collection by adding information from elsewhere. Clearly, networked information between different cultural institutions enhances the scope for research on item level. Examples include the work on *Codex Sinaiticus* (2010) and the work of the European Commission to combine Europe's multicultural and multilingual heritage in *Europeana* (2010) on a collection level. In addition, digitization coupled with other optical technology enables information to be read and interpreted in new ways, further advancing research, for example the Walters Art Museum's work on the *Archimedes Palimpsest* (2008). Lastly, new ways of using and looking at the collection have opened up through combining it with other available information, for example the use of geo-referencing in Tate's *Art Map* project (2010).

As online presentation offers the possibility to put together content in any conceivable way, there is great scope to develop specific education packages, directly supporting national or even international school curricula, for example, in the UK, The National Archives Education Service (www.nationalarchives.gov.uk/education) and the Science Museum's classroom resources (www.sciencemuseum.org.uk/educators.aspx). At the same time, online presentation allows formerly inaccessible material, such as negatives and fragile documents, to be made accessible. This is also where digital access aids preservation, as digitization enables research without touching the original. On a higher level, digitization will help to raise the profile of an institution, as an online presence will raise awareness of the existence of a collection and bring great opportunities to market it. In addition, it is possible to develop strategic links with related institutions, and thus re-position the collection within a broader or brand new context.

There is ample evidence that the possibilities offered by digitization together with new technology has expanded the vision of institutions. There are several prominent examples of institutions that have redefined their goals with a view to digital technology.

- The Smithsonian Institution in the USA makes 'the increase and diffusion of knowledge' its mission within the strategic plan 2010–15, imagining 'access to all known information . . . with one touch of the screen' (Smithsonian Institution, 2010).
- The British Library's strategy for 2008–11 aims to 'advance the world's knowledge' through seven strategic priorities, five of which aim to either advance the British Library's digital infrastructure or use digitally available content of the Library (British Library, 2008).
- The Koninklijke Bibliotheek (National Library) of the Netherlands states as its mission to 'bring people and information together'. Three of its strategic priorities in 2010-13 relate to digital content, with the top priority being to offer 'everyone access to everything published in and about the Netherlands' (Koninklijke Bibliotheek, 2010).
- The National Archives and Records Administration (NARA) of the USA revised their strategy in 2009 and aim to make their 'holdings and diverse programs available to more people than ever before through modern technology and dynamic partnerships' (National Archives and Records Administration, 2009).
- The National Archives of Australia (NAA) states in its corporate plan 2009–12 that it will 'continue to explore ways in which technological developments can enhance access to our collections' (National Archives of Australia, 2009).

Commercial partnerships have since developed in this sector, especially where the scale of the task makes internal resourcing impossible and the content is attractive to publishers and other online providers. The most noteworthy examples within the library sector are Google Book Search and Microsoft Live Books, whose aim it was to create searchable databases of full-text books (Rieger, 2008, 4–9). Archives, on the other hand, have taken advantage of the increasing interest in genealogy, and embarked on commercial partnerships focusing on family history content (e.g. partnerships with companies such as Ancestry, Brightsolid or FamilySearch). The advantages of teaming up with commercial partners in both cases are that digitization, including transcription, online presentation and marketing are resourced through the commercial partner, while the institution will get a copy of the scanned images. It can also provide a steady revenue stream as long as the demand for the digitized content remains strong. At the same time, digitizing cultural heritage collections benefits the private sector by stimulating new parts of the economy and encouraging creative thinking to develop new kinds of services using these images.

Commercial partnerships are not the only way that digitization projects are funded. Many grant-giving bodies will fund digitization and there are now specific funding streams dedicated to supporting institutions in their use of digital technologies; for example, the Joint Information Systems Committee (JISC) was set up in the UK to support education and research institutions by supplying funding and expertise. However, even grant-funded projects may have a commercial aspect if an institution uses a contractor to carry out the imaging and online delivery. Either way, the introduction of a commercial element adds new dimensions to collection management: an institution's staff may now need to work closely with a commercial company and the user may have to balance the cost of travelling to see the original against paying to see content online. Working with commercial partners is not inevitable but it is part of an overall shift in collection management and the way in which collections are used and accessed.

Collection management

The desire of libraries and archives to make books and documents more widely accessible fits into the need for accountability, especially where the spending of public money is involved. This has required collection managers to take a fresh look at all activities carried out within an institution. Waller (2003, 29–31) distinguishes three main processes in collection management:

1 The development of the collection through adding or removing items. This also includes activities such as processing, cataloguing, restoring and researching.
2 The use of the collection, which includes any activity benefiting from utilization of, reference to, information about, or the existence of the items contained within it.
3 The preservation of the collection with the aim of maintaining its value to an optimum level.

In all three processes, it is the value of the collection that is the focus of activity. Accessibility then forms the link between the collection, the values it represents and the specific process (see Figure 1.1). Collection management involves making well informed decisions in order to prioritize actions and optimize the allocation of resources to maintain as much accessible value as possible.

The development of digital technology and the opportunities that this has brought have created new challenges for the management of collections. For the conservator, who has traditionally focused their attention on preserving and developing the collection, emphasis is gradually shifting to *using* and

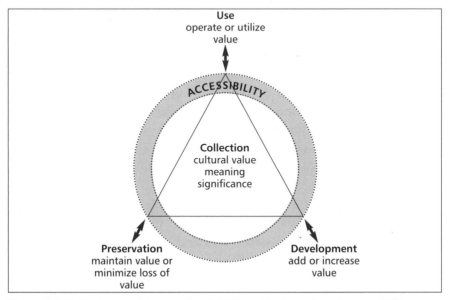

Figure 1.1 *Collection management triangle linking collection value with accessibility (Brokerhof et al., 2009)*

developing the collection. Preservation and use have thus far been seen as competing objectives; however, no library or archive keeps its collection just for the sake of keeping it. It is being kept with the expectation of being of value to current as well as future generations. Digitization has the potential to benefit both the development of a collection as well as its use. A well executed digitization project will result in detailed cataloguing information and metadata about a collection, while enhancing possibilities for its use in ways previously not conceived.

Doing this in a way that is sustainable, and that therefore benefits the preservation of the collection, as described in this publication, requires a pragmatic, risk-based approach from the collection manager. In addition, flexibility and the ability to understand the competing requirements of all interested parties, including commercial partners where those are involved, are pivotal in successfully balancing the preservation needs of the collection with the drive to make as much information as accessible as possible.

Access to content and context

There has been a long tradition amongst librarians and archivists to select and keep books and documents for the information they contain – information that was considered to add value to the collection as a whole within its specific context. Some items may have been selected for aesthetic reasons, such as the artistic value in their illuminations (even if the text could not be read or understood), but often little if any value has been attributed to aspects of their physical form, e.g. paper, parchment or media; or format, e.g. folding techniques, binding techniques or binding styles. At the same time, conservators have primarily focused on material attributes only, assuring readability and the ability to handle the object, while often staying oblivious to the content and context of an object.

Within the context of ever increasing digital possibilities, there are two seemingly opposing trends in the management of collections: on the one hand the desire to increase access to books and documents through online presentation, which conveys only the information and none of the material aspects, and, on the other to conserve material integrity as far as possible by carrying out less interventive conservation treatments, with the aim to preserve material as well as conceptual and contextual value for users now and in the future. However, although these trends may seem to conflict, they actually facilitate and complement each other. If a collection is available online, then the original documents are handled less and there is consequently less need for interventive treatments to keep them robust. In this way online access is in line with an overall trend in conservation towards minimal intervention. For the digital user there is a trade-off: they have the convenience of accessing the digital collection online from their own home, but they see a digital image and so do not experience the physical document. In the future the growing emphasis on the virtual rather than the material may result in a loss of appreciation of the material itself, or conversely the opposite may happen – as experiences become predominantly virtual there may be a growing reverence for the material world. The long-term effects remain to be seen (Nichols and Smith, 2001).

There are now two different ways to access collections: i) a single user can gain direct access to the physical object within the reading rooms of an institution, or, but possibly at the same time; ii) multiple users may have indirect access to the virtual object through online platforms. In order to make an item physically accessible to a reader, an institution not only has to have it listed and described within its catalogue, it also needs to have appropriate retrieval systems in place to allow it to be found within the repositories and delivered to the reading room. Without an entry in a catalogue, a potential user has no way of knowing of an item's existence within the collection; without internal retrieval systems, staff are unable to locate and deliver it. Both of these systems are therefore absolutely pivotal to making a collection accessible. In contrast, indirect access through the virtual, digitized item does not require any physical provisions through the originating institution. However, it must not be forgotten that appropriate systems need to be in place for online presentation in order to satisfy the needs of a user. The information needs to be indexed, tagged with keywords or similar, and the hosting institution will have to ensure that digital systems are operating at appropriate capacity to allow virtual presentation. In return, an institution may exploit the possibility of increasing the knowledge about their collection through using the collective knowledge of the research community within their virtual presentation platforms, for example The National Archives UK's wiki site (http://yourarchives.nationalarchives.gov.uk).

It has been suggested that digitization will make the need to facilitate direct access to documents through reading rooms redundant in future. Ramsholt (2009) suggests that digitization will result in a decline in reading room visitor numbers. However, the picture is not consistent. The National Archives UK, for example, had put over 80 million documents online by 2009 and while within a single month up to 12 million images might be downloaded, the number of document deliveries to the reading rooms – approximately 50,000 per month – has not declined but rather has remained constant. In fact, it has been shown that online presentation tends to generate interest and people who would previously not have thought of coming to the archive will now be drawn to visit. Strategic considerations to digitize the ten most popular record series would account for less than 20% of the total number of documents delivered into the reading rooms over the course of a year. At the same time, reducing document deliveries through this level of digitization has been estimated to require about six times the current annual operating budget of The National Archives UK, while the remaining 80% of physical document deliveries into the reading rooms would still need to be resourced. A further difficulty is that these 80% are often documents required by specialists such as journalists and academics – as opposed to the more predictable requests made by genealogists – and are therefore impossible to predict and pre-empt through digitization (Morley, 2009).

Planning and processing with minimal risk

Often, the value of cultural heritage is measured by the level of participation or use, resulting in an emphasis on numbers. This favours items for digitization which are of interest to many over those which might benefit for preservation reasons (de Lusenet, 2004). In addition, the idea that digital images constitute a preservation copy in a similar way that microfilm does has been disputed, mainly due to the uncertainties of digital preservation (Hughes, 2004, 8). As long as the challenges of digital preservation have not been fully met, digitization of any book or document cannot be seen as a preservation measure for the original itself. However, digitization projects will still help to improve the long-term prospects of a collection. The availability of digital copies reduces handling of the original, while an imaging project can be an opportunity to carry out rehousing or improve storage conditions. So while digitization is unlikely to solve all the problems of preservation there can be tangible benefits.

Alongside the preservation benefits there are, however, risks associated with the imaging process. The process must be sympathetic to the document, causing as little damage as possible. Experience so far has shown that it is highly likely that access to the original will be required again, be it for access to information and material in the near future, or for re-imaging projects in the medium or long term. Image capture does not need to cause damage. There have been ample examples of extremely carefully considered projects over the years, for example, the Special Collections at the University Library Graz (2010), digitization of the *Lindisfarne Gospels* for the online gallery at the British Library (2010) and digitization of the *Book of Kells* at Trinity College Dublin (2010). In all cases, digitization involved either single manuscripts or small parts of a special collection. Yet the required throughput of projects involving thousands or even millions of pages does pose risks to the documents: equipment itself may cause damage, and high-volume handling and time pressures can necessitate working processes that may compromise best practice. The resulting relatively minor damage must be weighed against the many benefits to be gained from digitization and this balancing act is at the heart of the collection manager's approach.

A fact that is often overlooked is that the documents themselves can pose challenges to the image capture operation. There is a risk that the capture rate is tortuously slow because of the need for careful unpacking and unfolding, or that the resulting images may not capture all information because documents are damaged. In the worst case scenario image capture may have to stop altogether if documents are found to be contaminated with mould, or are too damaged to be handled. These scenarios can be anticipated and managed with careful, well informed planning that involves the input of a collection manager. The key role of the collection manager is to consider the physical attributes of the items, and how these attributes will influence the imaging operation. Experience has shown that it is essential that the collection manager is involved from the outset so that the planning of the imaging operation takes into account the nature of the physical items and their preservation requirements. The role of the collection manager is therefore very much that of a facilitator, using their skills and knowledge to ensure the smooth running of the imaging operation while minimizing the risk to the documents.

The collection manager is not necessarily a conservator, but there are certainly parts of the project that require a conservator's skills and knowledge, in particular when assessing the condition of items and when preparing damaged items for imaging. Approaches to conservation differ according to the context, and a digitization project requires an approach that balances the need to address damage and the need for expediency, since projects often have tight budgets and timescales. In practice this means that interventive work is kept to a minimum and that treatments may be adapted and carried out in batches to maximize efficiency. Likewise, the documentation of treatments may be kept to a minimum. Since every digitization project is different it may be appropriate to adapt the treatment according to the type of equipment used. As previously mentioned, this overall approach is in keeping with current trends towards minimal intervention in conservation, except that in the context of the digitization project, the conservator must consider the way in which the items will be handled during imaging and the need for all information to be captured. These themes, concerning practical aspects of a digitization project, run through the following chapters of the book.

The four phases of digitization

In order to meet the objectives of both preserving a collection and increasing access to it, it is essential to acknowledge and plan for all phases of digitization projects from the very beginning through to the very end. A framework for such projects has been suggested by Rieger (2008, 16) and the Public Record Office Victoria (2010), although activities can be grouped into four distinct phases (see Figure 1.2). From this model it is apparent that image capture is only one part of a complex process.

Phase one

Phase one includes the selection of material (see Chapter 4 'The process of selection'), anticipating its use as well as assessing any copyright issues,

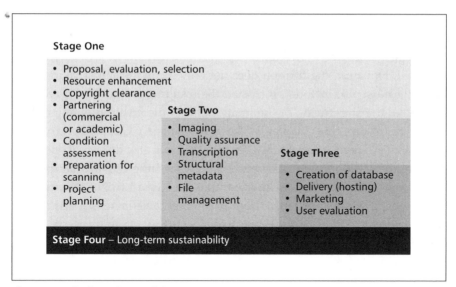

Figure 1.2 *The four phases of digitization*

which might be the deciding factor for some projects. At this point it is also necessary to consider the funding of the project, as digitization requires considerable financial resources. The content of the collection may point towards external funding sources. Any commercial company interested in selling digitized content will have a very specific remit, and therefore specific content will potentially attract specific commercial companies. For example, archival documents containing people's names and whereabouts might interest companies specializing in family history. Equally, there might be academic partners willing to fund projects if content furthers their learning and research aims, or grant sources where digitization fulfils the main remit of the funder. Equally, preservation may be the primary driver for a funder to grant money. Phase one will include a statistical survey of the collection by a collection manager or conservator to assess physical attributes so as to inform resource requirements and aid project planning. At this point, a decision regarding how to prepare documents for scanning will be made. This phase may therefore include the preparation of documents by a conservator, where it is possible to do so in advance.

Phase two

The second phase of a digitization project includes the actual image capture, the stage where the collection manager or conservator will be heavily involved. However, digitization does not only mean the actual taking of an image, it must also include processing the resulting images, the creation of metadata, the structuring of the image set and the creation of an archival master set of files (see Chapter 3 'The digital image'). Quality control must also be built in here. It should include, first, the control of the actual operation from a preservation point of view, ensuring as little damage as possible occurs, and, second, must include rigorous quality control of the resulting images, as it is more efficient to re-take unacceptable images while having the documents still at hand. Phase two may also include transcription or optical character recognition (OCR), where this is possible and desired.

Phase three

Phase three will consist of preparing the dataset for online presentation. There is also likely to be an element of website development for presenting the actual product as well as marketing and promoting it. Lastly, it should include incorporation of user feedback where possible, and the set up of ongoing user support. If digitization was carried out within the context of a commercial enterprise, then charging and related financial aspects will need to be set up and managed. This third phase already contains aspects that are ongoing, such as marketing and managing finances. These aspects must be recognized from the start; simply owning a set of digital images will not make information any more available than not having them digitized. Digitization will always result in long-term financial implications for the originating institution.

Phase four

Phase four has to be seen in this context, because sustaining the collection for most institutions will involve the management and financing of long-term preservation of the digital images as well as the originals. The preservation benefits of online access will only last as long as the digital images are available for online users. When collection managers consider the preservation of their physical collections they typically think in terms of the next 100 years. As yet, there is still no certainty regarding the feasibility of the preservation of digital surrogates over such a time span, nor is there reliable data on the cost of digital preservation, even though current trends suggest that digital technology will become cheaper over the course of time (Chapman, 2003; Palm, 2005). Planning to keep digital content accessible for at least ten years should be feasible, but the resource requirements for maintaining a digital collection might even be higher than the continuing preservation needs of the original. At the same time, new technologies will continue to evolve, making it likely that collections will be redigitized, exploiting new optical possibilities in the same way that collections currently available as black and white microfilm surrogates are now getting digitized in full colour; and even items previously digitized are being redigitized in order to allow, for example, for 'turning the pages' technology. In the face of these developments, it is all the more important to balance the need for widened access to information with the preservation of the original, as the idea of a never-to-be-touched original has already been proven wrong.

Fitting digitization into collection management

There are some significant benefits for collection management brought on by digitization projects: the intensive work, especially when involving large parts of the collection, goes hand in hand with the acquisition of new knowledge about it. Materials and typical damage phenomena become apparent, which can feed into strategic aims for the collection. Equally, every digitization project results in improved cataloguing and metadata about this part of the collection, which in turn will enhance access and help to preserve the original by ensuring that staff find the desired item without much searching and the reader can see exactly what they were looking for.

Managing a collection in terms of its preservation, use and development, the contribution of digitization is two-fold (see Figure 1.3): digitization will help to preserve the collection by maintaining the value of the collection through a reduction in access to the original and allowing it to be stored more cost-effectively in terms of storage location and environment, where possible; at the same time, digitization allows the information contained within a book or document to be made accessible online on a much broader basis, therefore

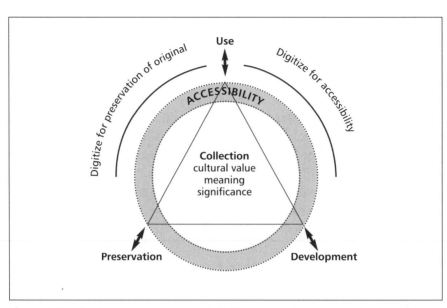

Figure 1.3 *Collection management triangle linking preservation, use and development through digitization (Brokerhof et al., 2009)*

supporting the use of the collection. It is for these reasons that digitization should be fully embedded within any collection management strategy, involving those charged with the preservation of the collection as well as those charged with making it accessible to the user.

Chapter summary

- Institutions can reach new audiences through online access, which also presents opportunities to build connections with other institutions. Online resources can utilize new technologies and provide a wealth of contextual information. Digitization aids the preservation of a collection by reducing the handling of the originals.
- Digitization might introduce a commercial element that is part of an overall shift in collection management that places more emphasis on the use and development of collections.
- Digitization is not in conflict with preservation but can complement and facilitate it. However, in the long term it is unlikely to result in an overall reduction in demand for access to original documents and is not a solution for

all preservation problems.

- Image capture can be done on a small scale without causing damage but in a large project, when thousands of documents are processed, some handling damage is inevitable. The collection manager must be involved at an early stage not only to ensure document welfare but also to ensure the smooth running of the operation. Physical attributes of the documents will influence the image capture operation.
- Digitization should be embedded in an institution's collection management strategy because it brings benefits to the preservation, use and development of the collection.

Bibliography

The Archimedes Palimpsest Project (2008) *The Imaging of the Archimedes Palimpsest,* www.archimedespalimpsest.org/imaging_initialtrials1.html.

British Library (2008) *The British Library's Strategy 2008–2011,* www.bl.uk/aboutus/stratpolprog/strategy0811/strategysummary.pdf.

British Library (2010) *Online Gallery: sacred texts: Lindisfarne Gospels,* www.bl.uk/onlinegallery/sacredtexts/lindisfarne.html.

Brokerhof, A. W., Ankersmit, B., Chin-a-Fo, J., Luger, T. and Scholte, T. (2009) *Values and Criteria: towards a mother model for valuation of cultural heritage,* Instituut Collectie Nederland, internal discussion paper.

Chapman, S. (2003) Counting the Costs of Digital Preservation: is repository storage affordable?, *Journal of Digital Information,* **4** (2), article 178, http://journals.tdl.org/jodi/article/view/100/99.

Codex Sinaiticus (2010) *Codex Sinaiticus: participants,* www.codexsinaiticus.org/en/project/participants.aspx.

de Lusenet, Y. (2004) *Keeping Things that Work: preservation aspects of digitization,* EURESCO Conference on 'Philological Disciplines and Digital Technologies: computational philology: tradition versus innovation' (Il Ciocco, 6–11 September 2003), www.knaw.nl/ecpa/publ/ciocco.pdf.

Europeana (2010) *Think Culture,* www.europeana.eu/portal/index.html.

Hughes, L. (2004) *Digitizing Collections: strategic issues for the information manager,* Facet Publishing.

Koninklijke Bibliotheek (2010) *Strategic Plan 2010–2013,*

www.kb.nl/bst/beleid/bp/2010/index-en.html.

Morley, O. (2009) *Digitisation and Our Options for The National Archives Future Strategy*, The National Archives UK, internal presentation.

National Archives and Records Administration (2009) *Preserving the Past to Protect the Future: the strategic plan of the National Archives and Records Administration, 2006–2016, revised 2009,*
www.archives.gov/about/plans-reports/strategic-plan/2009/nara-strategic-plan-2009-2016-update.pdf.

National Archives of Australia (2009) *Corporate Plan 2009–2012,*
www.naa.gov.au/Images/CorporatePlan2009-10to2011-12_tcm2-28444.pdf.

Nichols, S. G. and Smith, A. (2001) *The Evidence in Hand: report of the task force on the artifact in library collections*, Council on Library and Information Resources.

Palm, J. (2005) *The Digital Black Hole,*
www.tape-online.net/docs/Palm_Black_Hole.pdf.

Public Record Office Victoria (2010) *Digitization Requirements*, PROS 10/02, Specification 1, www.prov.vic.gov.au/publications/publns/1002s1.pdf.

Ramsholt, K. J. (2009) Digitization: threat or benefit to conservation?, *Journal of Paper Conservation*, **10** (2), 21–4.

Rieger, O. Y. (2008) *Preservation in the Age of Large-scale Digitization*, Council on Library and Information Resources.

Smithsonian Institution (2010) *Inspiring Generations through Knowledge and Discovery,*
www.si.edu/about/documents/SI_Strategic_Plan_2010-2015.pdf.

Tate (2010) *Art Map*, www.tate.org.uk/artmap.

Trinity College Dublin (2010) *The Old Library & the Book of Kells Exhibition,*
www.bookofkells.ie/book-of-kells.

University Library Graz (2010) *Special Collections,*
www.uni-graz.at/ubwww/ub-sosa/ub-sosa-handschriften.htm.

Waller, R. R. (2003) *Cultural Property Risk Analysis Model*, Acta Universitatis Gothoburgensis.

2

Before you digitize: resources, suppliers and surrogates

Introduction

As seen in Chapter 1 'Digitization in the context of collection management', digitization is much more than simply image capture. Managing digitization projects involves managing numerous technical, legal and logistical issues. The many aspects of project management are beyond the scope of this book, but are covered in detail by Hughes (2004).

When embarking on digitization there are a number of fundamental issues that need to be considered before individual projects are initiated. Many of these issues concern the preservation of the collection and so the collection manager must ensure that they are included in the decision-making process. The issues discussed here are: the implications for an institution's resources; the pros and cons of outsourcing; and the role of microfilm.

Impact on the institution

A digitization programme, like any major new initiative, will have an impact on the resources of an institution. It must be recognized that digitization projects are complex and that they require contributions from a number of different experts. Even if externally funded through grants, commercial or academic partnerships, they will require a library or archive to rethink their priorities in order to dedicate enough internal resources (Bülow, 2009). Staff who might be involved with such projects include:

- curators and archivists
- copyright experts

- procurement staff or legal advisors
- conservators
- scanning operators or imaging experts
- IT support staff
- digital preservation experts
- public-facing staff who are familiar with the needs of users
- marketing and press staff.

Inevitably not all institutions will have experts in all of these fields. Where internal experts are not available, a library or archive might need to think of alternative ways of getting advice, which may come at a cost; see Hughes (2004, 104–6) for other sources of expertise. For an institution wishing to implement an extensive digitization programme it is worth investing in existing staff so that they can acquire some of the necessary skills. When staff develop a specialism in digitization the impact is that departmental priorities and work plans might have to be adjusted to allow time for their involvement in digitization projects. The advantage of developing in-house expertise is that this will help to ensure that the digitization programme can remain sustainable in the long term.

Impact on the conservation studio

Digitization that involves image capture from original documents will require in-house conservation resources. The approach strongly advocated by this book is that conservation staff must be involved with digitization projects from the outset. This involvement is required at different levels: senior staff may be needed for strategic decisions and resourcing issues while collection surveys and preparation of documents may be carried out by conservation assistants or technicians under the supervision of a conservator. It should therefore be recognized that a digitization project may need contributions from a range of conservation staff.

The conservation requirements of each project will vary according to the needs of the documents, for example, Lindsay (2003) describes several different projects carried out at the London Metropolitan Archives, each requiring differing degrees of document preparation. One of the projects included disbinding, which was carried out by conservation assistants, while another involved the treatment of mould, which was carried out by conservators. The work carried out at London Metropolitan Archives was intended simply to stabilize the documents and prepare them for imaging and so was not full conservation treatment, but the nature of the work was still highly labour intensive, for example, over a 15-month period three conservation assistants prepared 400 volumes.

If more than one digitization project is implemented at the same time the implications for conservation resources can be tremendous. Since the preparation of documents can result in a large quantity of items passing through the studio, there may need to be special provision for secure storage, additional work surfaces for bulk treatments and special arrangements for the delivery and return of batches of items. Other projects may need to be put on hold and additional staff may be needed. Conservation resources should therefore be carefully planned so that support for digitization projects is managed and is balanced with other conservation activities.

This assumes that the in-house conservation studio has sufficient resources to support digitization projects, but this might not always be the case. There may be an overwhelming amount of digitization work that a studio cannot accommodate or staff may already be committed to other projects. Another consideration is that preparing documents for digitization, generally involving minimal treatments, is not necessarily the best use of time for highly skilled conservators when there are other activities to be carried out. It could be the case that once a digitization programme is launched the preparation of documents for digitization becomes the dominant activity and the studio becomes less of a conservation department and more of a workshop for document preparation.

While some conservators may baulk at this thought, others are concerned that once documents are digitized the need for conservation (and therefore conservators) is diminished. This has stimulated some debate within the conservation profession. A questionnaire circulated amongst Norwegian paper conservators in 2006 found that the majority viewed digitization as a threat (Ramsholt, 2009). However, digitization can also be an opportunity to reassess the role of the conservator since conservation projects no longer need to be prioritized on the basis of the popularity of the records if the most popular records are available online. Vervoorst argues in favour of a move towards 'deterioration-based collection mapping' with an emphasis on identifying inherently unstable material (2008, 176). Conservators can also be more proactively engaged with collection development through technical examination and conservation research, and by disseminating their knowledge more widely. With the growth of digitization there remains an undoubted role for the conservator in collection management but the conservation profession must evolve as the strategic landscape shifts.

Use of project conservators

Collection surveys are essential for planning conservation resources because they provide estimates of the conservation work required for each digitization project. Resources can then be allocated to individual projects on a case-by-case basis. This can be done by deploying existing staff but another option is to employ project conservators to supplement the existing resources. It may be possible to fund temporary project conservators out of the project budget since, logically, the conservation work is a project cost. If this is agreed from the inception of the project then costs for conservation work can be included in the initial business case or grant application. If adopting this approach then a collection survey should be carried out at an early stage (see Chapter 5 'Surveying collections').

Having a conservator dedicated to a particular digitization project has many advantages, regardless of whether they are a member of the temporary project staff or existing conservation staff. A conservator dedicated to one project will not be distracted by other commitments. Also, the project conservator can have a multifaceted role, carrying out preservation training for the imaging team and responding to their ad hoc queries. The project conservator can be responsible for the document ordering and tracking, documentation and reporting, and can be a single point of contact for the project manager. As can be seen in the case studies in Chapter 8 'Preparation of damaged documents', the conservation work is often run in parallel to the imaging operation necessitating close collaboration between the imaging team and the conservator. Having a single point of contact simplifies the lines of communication.

Lastly, an important but less tangible benefit is that if newly recruited temporary staff are used they can bring a fresh dynamic to the conservation studio. This type of project work is ideally suited to recent conservation graduates who have the relevant skills and knowledge but may lack much experience of bench work. Newly qualified staff will bring a fresh perspective and may introduce new ideas and ways of working to the studio. This should not be underestimated in a profession that strives for continual development.

Choosing to outsource
The pros and cons of outsourcing

If an institution lacks in-house facilities for digitization it may seem that the only option is to outsource the digitization to a commercial company. A commercial supplier will have the relevant expertise and technical knowledge. Being a specialist they are more likely to have state-of-the-art equipment and appropriately trained staff and so should be able to offer a very competitive price for their services. This is certainly an attractive option for an institution for whom digitization is a one-off venture because it will be more cost effective than purchasing expensive equipment. At the other end of the scale, an institution can use several different suppliers to run several digitization projects at the same time within a short timeframe.

Gertz (2000) provides an introductory framework for finding and approaching suppliers – a potentially daunting prospect given the range of services offered by information management companies. However, a single supplier may not provide all of the services that are required, so a digitization project may involve more than one contract; for example, image capture and transcription may be carried out by two different companies. Alternatively, the supplier may subcontract a service to a third party. This need not be a problem if the project is well managed.

A more serious concern, probably of more significance to the collection manager than the project manager, is that although there are currently many companies who offer digitization services there are still relatively few who have worked with the heritage sector. Suppliers without such experience of this sector may not appreciate the priorities and concerns of the institution. For its part, the institution is likely to have dealt with commercial companies before (perhaps on publishing or marketing projects) but image capture involves the processing of original items and as such requires a close working relationship with the supplier to ensure that requirements on both sides are understood and met.

Working with suppliers

During a digitization project, the cultural institution and the commercial company will share a common goal – the creation of the digital copy. However, there are fundamental differences between the two sides which can result in conflicting requirements. These differences can be summarized as follows.

- *Different values*. The institution will have some core values that are not shared by the supplier. Most significant of these is the importance of the preservation of the collection, but transparency and accountability may also be important. For the supplier, one of the main priorities will be cost-effectiveness so as to maximize their profit, and preservation of the original items may be an alien concept.
- *Different expectations*. If the supplier has no previous experience of a heritage collection they may be completely unprepared for the nature of the material itself, especially its diversity and idiosyncrasies. They may struggle to adapt to the challenges.
- *Administration*. An institution must document its work so as to be accountable to stakeholders and is also likely to have procedures and systems in place for everything from stationery orders to parking permits. To a supplier this can be cumbersome and may cause delays.

In order to build a successful working relationship both sides must be prepared to learn from each other and to adapt their approach. The institution must accept that, when they hand over the original items to the supplier, there is a risk of some damage occurring during processing. It is not feasible to eliminate all risks. The supplier, for their part, would gain from learning more about their client and their client's background so as to understand the context of the project. This may help them to be more sympathetic to the institution's needs.

The collection manager and the conservator will be in the front line of the working relationship because they will need to work very closely with the supplier to ensure that equipment and processes are appropriate. They should also be involved throughout the imaging operation to provide ad hoc guidance to the imaging team should any issues arise. However, in general, there are some points to bear in mind when working with a supplier.

- Be prepared. Carry out a collection survey and share the information with the supplier so that both sides are fully informed and know what to expect from the documents.
- Keep communication open and clear. From the beginning have one point of contact for the supplier. Establish regular progress meetings if necessary. Avoid jargon and acronyms. Always seek to ensure that both sides understand and agree the issues that have been discussed. If the supplier uses technical language then ask for clarification.
- Keep administration to a minimum and avoid unnecessary paperwork.
- Be flexible. The institution will have minimum requirements, especially where document welfare is concerned, but should remain open to the supplier's suggestions. Don't move the goalposts. Both sides have a duty to inform the other if something changes. If the institution changes the scope of the project then they should be aware that this will have an impact on the supplier.
- Monitor the situation and raise any concerns early. Likewise be prepared to respond to any issues promptly.

Overall, the aim should be to facilitate the project, not obstruct, and so the collection manager should in the first instance aim to be accommodating while not forgetting the bottom line, which is that the documents should not be put at undue risk (Ahmon, Bülow and Kimbell, 2008).

The benefits of in-house digitization

Outsourcing is not the only option. If an institution has the appetite to undertake a programme of digitization it is worth considering setting up in-house image capture facilities or converting a microfilming operation to a digital one. There are several examples of institutions establishing dedicated scanning facilities to enable digitization on a large scale. One of the earliest institutions to do this was the National Archives of Sweden. Its Media Conversion Centre (*Mediakonverteringscentrum*; MKC) started off in 1991 as a microfilming facility, introducing digitization in 1996 and completing the shift to digitization in 2003. This facility employs 62 staff including conservators, imaging operators and technical staff. Interestingly, this facility digitizes not only government-owned material, but also operates on a commercial basis

(Palm, 2010; Riksarkivet, 2010). Similarly, the National Library of Finland founded the Centre for Preservation and Digitisation in 1990 and employs 50 staff focusing on the creation of surrogates. In Finland, both microfilming and digitization are currently carried out (National Library of Finland, 2010).

The main advantage of an in-house facility is that the institution has complete control and does not need to work with an external party. Also, unlike a contractual agreement with a supplier, there is a degree of flexibility so that if requirements change over time the operation can be adapted. This can be particularly important in the early days. Over time, using the same in-house facilities and staff gives continuity to successive projects and ensures a consistent approach, building on the skills and experience of staff. The importance of staff development is a point stressed by Hughes (2004, 96–104), particularly in a time of profound change in libraries and archives and restrictions on resources.

On-site or off-site?

It is not necessarily the case that an in-house operation is on-site and an outsourced operation is off-site. If an institution has the on-site space and resources then it is preferable to set up the image capture operation on-site even if the imaging is outsourced. An external supplier can install their own equipment and staff on-site, and the host may be able to recover the cost of space rental and infrastructure from them.

From a preservation perspective, the advantages of setting up an operation on-site are clear – the operation can utilize existing systems for document ordering, delivery, storage and security and all relevant support staff are already in place. The collection manager can have the reassurance of knowing that documents remain within the institution and they can readily monitor the operation and respond immediately to any issues that arise. This not only satisfies preservation concerns, but is also simpler from a logistical point of view. However, if the on-site resources cannot accommodate an image capture operation then an off-site facility might be the only option. Alternatively, if image capture is being outsourced, the supplier may already have an established off-site facility that they would like to use.

When planning to carry out image capture off-site the institution must ensure that the standards of care which are adhered to on-site are also upheld at the off-site location and during transit. When working with a supplier it will be necessary to define these standards so that the minimum requirements are clear to both sides. It will also be necessary to carry out a site inspection to assess the facility and services and, if possible, to carry out periodic inspections to monitor the situation. There are many factors to consider, both in terms of preservation and logistics. An overview of the key factors is given below. Chapter 9 'Setting up the imaging operation' deals with setting up a work area in more detail.

Environmental conditions

Most cultural institutions are striving to maintain certain environmental conditions according to the appropriate best practice guidelines or standards. These will mainly concern light levels, temperature and relative humidity (RH). It is best practice to minimize light exposure during storage. Archives and libraries will also aim to keep the temperature relatively low, and RH relatively stable and below 65%. While each institution might have its own idea of these requirements, it is important to balance the needs of the collection, the imaging operation and the project staff. For example, it may be reasonable to decide on minimum acceptable conditions, rather than imposing strict ranges, since the off-site storage is temporary and documents may be stored there for only a few weeks. A building with inadequate environmental control will not be suitable but can be adapted by, for example, covering windows and improving insulation. Continuous monitoring of the environment should be in place so that the environment can be assessed. Standards for the storage environment will also include guidelines for fire resistance and storage furniture, so a thorough site visit would be a good way to assess its suitability.

Incident plan and security

Having a robust incident plan is standard practice in collection management and any site that will house part of the institution's collection should have appropriate plans in place in the event of an incident. Needless to say, security measures must be in place in order to minimize the risk of loss or theft. Items must be insured and this should be clarified before any documents are transported off-site. The security of the building and site, along with staff security clearance and the security of delivery vehicles, must be taken into account.

Transport and tracking

Transport and tracking systems must be robust so as to ensure the security and welfare of the documents. For example, it may be a requirement that items are delivered directly from the institution to the off-site location without stopping anywhere else on the route, and that there are two drivers at any time. Items must be adequately packed before dispatch and this will require resources at both locations, including packing materials (e.g. boxes, crates) and staff time. It may be possible to adapt the existing document tracking system for off-site use. If a new system is being developed then this should be compatible with the existing one so that document moves can be tracked smoothly.

Workflow

A robust system is needed to ensure a steady supply of items to and from the off-site location. Workflow can be problematic if some documents need the attention of a conservator. This is a critical issue because if there are difficulties imaging the documents then without on-site support the operation can be seriously hampered. The options for incorporating conservation work into the workflow are dealt with in Chapter 8 'Preparation of damaged documents', but the best approach for an off-site operation may be to employ a project conservator to provide full-time support. This would involve setting up a workspace for the conservator, which would need to include work surfaces, a water source, good lighting and some simple equipment.

The role of microfilm

Both digital and microfilm copies contribute to preservation by providing access without the need to handle the original documents. However, while the longevity of microfilm seems assured, there remain doubts over the long-term longevity of digital files. At present therefore there is still a role for microfilm at many institutions.

Film as a preservation medium

It was the *Convention for the Protection of Cultural Property in the Event of Armed Conflict* adopted at The Hague (Netherlands) of 1954, which boosted the use of microfilming by stipulating to 'prepare in time of peace for the safeguarding of cultural property . . . against the foreseeable effects of an armed conflict, by taking such measures as [are] appropriate' (Hague Convention, 1954). Institutions use microfilm to preserve their most vulnerable and most valuable collections, the principle being that if the originals are destroyed or lost the microfilm copy will survive. Microfilm seems a suitable preservation medium as its relative permanence has been proven over the last 150 years or so and there are now well established standards in place. Also, institutions may already have in-house filming facilities with staff who have many years of expertise in filming.

Digitization offers the allure of high resolution colour images but compared with microfilm the technology is still developing. In particular, there are still issues around the preservation of digital surrogates with the result that major institutions are not yet prepared to use it for preservation copying (for example, see British Library, 2008). Making the switch from microfilming to digital imaging is costly both in terms of capital expenditure and staff retraining. Even if digital preservation issues are resolved, microfilm may be preferable because it is likely to be cheaper to produce and to maintain. It has been estimated that the preservation of digital images costs about three times as much as the storage of microfilm or original material (Chapman, 2005).

The hybrid approach

Since the late 1980s, the demise of microfilm has been predicted (Weber, 1998). Today, digital surrogates undoubtedly offer advantages over microfilm as a medium for access, but the industry remains optimistic about the future of microfilm and is now actively promoting it as a preservation medium (Negus, 2007). The impact on digitization is that microfilm is likely to remain the preferred preservation medium and if microfilm is embedded in the preservation strategy of an institution there may be a requirement to generate a microfilm copy for preservation as well as a digital copy for access. For example, the TIDEN project, co-ordinated by the Helsinki University Library, concerned the Nordic newspaper collections from several national and state libraries. The collections were microfilmed for preservation purposes and then the microfilm was digitized in order to provide online access (Bremer-Laamanen, 2003). The creation of two surrogates results in a triple set of records to be kept and this can be a considerable drain on resources. Before adopting this hybrid approach an institution should therefore clarify how this sits with their preservation strategy.

The impact on image capture

From both a logistical and a preservation standpoint it is preferable to carry out imaging of a collection only once. The choice is therefore to either digitize and then generate film from the digital copy, or to microfilm and then digitize the film. There are specialist scanners available for digitizing microfilm and the imaging industry has now developed systems for digital to film conversion. However, the two approaches can differ in terms of the overall cost and the quality of the resulting image; see Lee (2000, 64–6) for an overview of these issues. The decision to film or digitize first will be determined by a combination of factors including existing resources and institutional expertise.

From a preservation point of view there is little difference between the assessment and preparation of collections for microfilming or for digitization as the principles are the same (Lindsay, 2003). However, systems for capturing digital images are varied and some systems will not be suitable for all document types. The collection manager may therefore need to be more involved at the project development stage with a digital image capture than with filming (see Chapter 6 'Equipment for image capture').

In some cases, microfilm of the collection might already exist and so the decision might be taken to digitize from the old film copy. This is not only much cheaper than digitizing the original documents, but it also saves having to handle and process the originals. Microfilm scanning is an automated process that can be carried out off-site by an information management company. Security and document welfare are secondary here, as the films are already surrogates, and the original usually still exists. However, the condition of the film should be checked, as well as the image quality. Microfilm from early mass-imaging projects may often exhibit poor image quality, which might lead to readers asking for the original. Also, the collection manager will need to decide whether it is appropriate to use the archival master copy of the microfilm, where scanning might pose risks of physical damage. Again, this decision should be made in the context of the institution's preservation strategy, balancing the potential for damage with the risk of a lower quality of digital image from the working master film.

Chapter summary

- Digitization projects require the involvement of a range of specialists. An institution should consider training existing staff and may need to seek advice from external consultants.
- The use of temporary project conservators offers a sustainable approach to planning conservation resources for digitization projects. Temporary project staff should be funded out of the project budget.
- An institution can tap into industry expertise by outsourcing to a commercial supplier, but handing the original documents to a supplier introduces risks and so the process must be carefully managed.
- Working with suppliers can be a steep learning curve. Be prepared and maintain good communication throughout the process.
- Conducting image capture on-site is preferable for logistical and preservation reasons. If the image capture is to take place off-site then minimum requirements must be set.
- Digital images offer enhanced access but microfilm remains the preferred preservation medium. Some institutions may want to capture both digital and film copies to satisfy the needs of preservation and access.

Bibliography

Ahmon, J., Bülow, A. E. and Kimbell, C. (2008) Balancing Preservation and Access with Commercial Interests. Paper presented at *Creative Collaborations: 36th Annual Meeting: April 21-24, 2008: Hyatt Regency Denver, Denver, CO., American Institute for Conservation of Historic and Artistic Works (AIC)*, unpublished.

Bremer-Laamanen, M. (2003) Digitization for Access to Preserved Documents, *Liber Quarterly*, **13** (2), 137–45.

British Library (2008) *Position Paper: preservation copying policy (microfilm to digital)*,
www.bl.uk/aboutus/stratpolprog/ccare/introduction/preservation/policy&position/Position%20Paper-Preservation%20Copying%20Policy.pdf.

Bülow, A. E. (2009) Business Models for Large-scale Digitisation Projects at The National Archives UK. Paper presented at *Digitizing for Preservation and Access: past is prologue: 23rd Annual Preservation Conference: March 26, 2009: National Archives building, Washington, DC.*,
www.archives.gov/preservation/conferences/2009/presentations.

Chapman, S. (2005) Microfilm: a preservation technology for the 21st Century? In Frey, F. and Buckley, R. (eds), *Archiving 2005: final program and proceedings, April 26–9, 2005, Washington DC*, Society for Imaging Science and Technology.

Gertz, J. (2000) Vendor Relations. In Sitts, M. K. (ed.), *Handbook for Digital Projects: a management tool for preservation and access: first edition*, Northeast Document Conservation Centre,
www.nedcc.org/resources/digitalhandbook/viii.htm.

Hague Convention (1954) *Convention for the Protection of Cultural Property in the Event of Armed Conflict*, www.icomos.org/hague.

Hughes, L. (2004) *Digitizing Collections: strategic issues for the information manager*, Facet Publishing.

Lee, S. (2000) *Digital Imaging: a practical handbook*, Library Association Publishing.

Lindsay, H. (2003) Preservation Microfilming and Digitization at London Metropolitan Archives: surveying and conservation preparation prior to image capture, *The Paper Conservator*, **27**, 47–57.

National Library of Finland (2010) *Centre for Preservation and Digitisation*, www.nationallibrary.fi/libraries/dimiko.html.

Negus, P. (2007) The Future of Microfilm. In Webster, J. and Reed, C. (eds), *Second Life for Collections: papers given at the National Preservation Office conference held 29 October 2007 at the British Library*, National Preservation Office.

Palm, J. (2010) personal communication.

Ramsholt, K. J. (2009) Digitization: threat or benefit to conservation? *Journal of Paper Conservation*, **10** (2), 21–4.

Riksarkivet (2010) *MKC: the complete solution*,
www.riksarkivet.se/default.aspx?id=19196&refid=1135.

Vervoorst, J. (2008) New Conservation Opportunities in a World of Digitization and Access. In Saunders, D., Townsend, J. H. and Woodcock, S. (eds), *Conservation and Access: contributions to the London Congress, 15–19 September 2008*, The International Institute for Conservation of Historic and Artistic Works.

Weber, H. (1998) *Der Mikrofilm im Archiv: Bestandsaufnahme und Zukunft*, www.uni-muenster.de/Forum-Bestandserhaltung/konversion/mikro-weber.html.

3

The digital image

Ross Spencer

Introduction

Developing a technical specification for digital images is one of the numerous issues alluded to in Chapter 2 'Before you digitize: resources, suppliers and surrogates'. The way in which the images are to be used will determine the specification of the digital files. Usage amongst other things affects decisions about access, storage and image quality. Performance requirements of a delivery mechanism might dictate one file format over another in the short term but planning might want to take into account the alternatives as time moves on and performance becomes less of an issue with more capable and more powerful computer systems.

Digital images available for widespread use complement academic research; they provide an unprecedented level of access to documents and objects where it might not normally be possible to get access or to view them in such great detail. In some cases, highlighted by Prescott (2008), digital images can reveal details that cannot be seen by the naked eye. Digital images mean that users are better able to study documents that edited manuscripts cannot provide and where handling the original comes at too great a cost to be allowed.

The best possible image must be available for study, and for preservation purposes it is important that redigitization should be done rarely, if at all. From that point of view the two objectives are mutually inclusive. Indeed, when you are digitizing records where the original paper copy is extremely fragile, physical access might be limited for very good reason and redigitizing might not physically be possible – and thus the best possible image specification and image capture must be outlined and achieved the first time around. This much is paramount.

Within this chapter we hope to cover the majority of the options available to those embarking on digitization projects including looking at the basic concepts of digital images, their use, the options available after processing and what choices digital curators are likely to have to make to give them a satisfactory result that will last long into the future. Specifics concerning the actual image capturing equipment are discussed in Chapter 6 'Equipment for image capture'.

Basic concepts

There are a number of basic concepts that define a digital image. The image might encapsulate a number of other features but the basic concepts of resolution, bit-depth/colour-depth and colour management make up the core of what we call a digital image and we need to understand these in order to understand their impact within a digital imaging project. We must also look at the concept of the archival master image and service copy. Archival masters are images taken directly from the digitization process. These will be of the highest quality and resolution and are used to derive other images. Service copies, also referred to as presentation copies, display versions or public-facing images, will be derived from the archival master but might vary in size and quality; the specification for any digital image will change considerably depending on its potential use. We begin our overview of image specifications by looking at resolution.

Resolution

Resolution describes the detail a digital image encodes. We discuss resolution using various terms – pixels per inch (PPI) and dots per inch (DPI), for example – and in dimensions such as 1024 x 768, making reference to the number of pixels horizontally and vertically (on, for example, a computer display). Pixels per inch describes the number of pixels that are used to represent one inch in the digital image. Dots per inch is a term that refers to the printed image, specifically relating to the number of ink dots printed out over the length of an inch on paper. The term is still found in common parlance, perhaps inaccurately, when referring to digital images, when what is actually meant is PPI.

If you look closely at a digital image, or printed image under a microscope you will see its core components, pixels or dots. An entire image is made up of these dots. If you focus on a portion of the image, the more dots that make up this portion the more detail it contains. It has higher fidelity on paper and on your computer screen. Higher resolution images usually means images with more detail. When capturing an image or a document at different resolutions you will find that eventually the difference in the amount of detail you can see in an image begins to trail off. One of the best methods to find the required resolution for your objects is to experiment with the settings on your scanner or camera to find the optimum setting.

Twycross (2008, 27) discusses the impact of having a good quality, high resolution scan when examining manuscripts in scholarly detail. Using a scan of 967 PPI, and a screen resolution of 1024 pixels x 768 pixels, a word, 'pagiaunt', that is 14.7 mm on the original manuscript can be enlarged to 172 mm on screen with 'no loss of clarity'. There is sufficient detail in the enlarged image to show the turns of the pen and the flow of the ink. In the case of Twycross (2008), it is described that this amount of detail, brought about by having a high enough resolution, provides an excellent tool for teaching palaeography (the study of ancient writing) and, at a more advanced level, identifying handwriting by different individuals.

Resolution also dictates the file size of your images. Without taking into account compression, a one-inch squared object scanned at 300 PPI using a 24-bit colour format which has three 8-bit colour components per pixel will result in an image 300 pixels by 300 pixels, resulting in a file size of 300 pixels x 300 pixels x 3 bytes per pixel, equalling 270,000 bytes, which is 263 kilobytes.

In terms of scanning resolution you want to capture as much information as possible but you might need to take into account disk space. It is easy to calculate using this technique so you can always know the optimum scan resolution for your needs whether they are detail, disk-space or a balance between the two. Compression will reduce these file sizes further. The degree of this reduction varies between images, but similar images will achieve (roughly) a similar amount of compression.

The final use of an image should be considered when thinking about resolution. For example, if you intend to print a digital image at some point and use a printing resolution of 300 DPI, up-scaling from a 200 DPI scan to 300 DPI will reduce the overall quality of the image. Scanning to print at the correct resolution will provide a better result, as will downscaling from a larger image. If it is known beforehand that a large output image is required then scanning at a higher resolution will provide a larger image even if no additional detail is seen. It depends on individual requirements, so no absolute approach exists for achieving what it is wanted in every situation.

Bit-depth/Colour-depth

Bit-depth, or colour-depth, was alluded to in the worked example above describing file size. Bit-depth describes the number of bits used by a computer to represent each individual pixel. A common bit-depth of 24-bits means that each pixel is represented using 24-bits (3 bytes). Each 24-bit pixel is made up of the colours red, green and blue, so 8-bits (1 byte) is used to represent each colour. A higher number of bits means larger file sizes, but it usually also means greater colour-depth.

Bit-depth might also refer to a colour's representation within an indexed colour image. Indexed colour images consist of a palette representing each distinct colour in an image. The pixels within the image representation then map to the location in the palette of the colour they are referring to. The number of bits in an indexed colour image depends on how many colours are needed; 8-bits can represent 256 unique colours whereas 16-bits can represent 65,536 colours.

It is unlikely that digitized images will use indexed colour. Most resultant images will be continuous-tone colour (described in more detail below). Images that are greyscale are closer to what we associate with black and white. Each pixel in a greyscale image represents just intensity information, the presence of light or not. Modern implementations of greyscale use 8-bits to represent 256 shades of grey and in this sense are similar to an indexed colour image.

The 24-bit representation above is an example of an RGB (Red, Green, Blue) image, or truecolour (The MathWorks, 2010). Truecolour represents the combination of red, green and blue intensities (brightness) to specify a colour in the RGB colour model. This is an alternative model to CMYK (Cyan, Magenta, Yellow and blacK) which essentially masks the brightness of white using different combinations of colours to recreate a different subset again typically represented using 32-bits. While the two spaces contain some of the same colours, the two are essentially different and represent a different range (gamut). The range of colours both models represent is smaller than the gamut of all visible colours.

Colour using a 24-bit depth is a standard supported by a wide range of file formats and applications. At 24-bits per pixel the implementation is capable of representing 2^{24} colours, approximately 16.7 million colours. Some formats may support a type of colour called deep colour. This is a representation using more bits to provide a wider colour gamut. While this might become a *de facto* standard in the future it should be observed that support for deep colour is not that wide outside of professional image editing suites and so alternatives should be considered.

Colour management

Colour management is an important concept that has a wider impact beyond the initial imaging phases of a project. While we will not discuss these uses in depth, colour management does need to be considered at each stage of the digitization workflow to ensure the highest quality product when an image is printed, for example, or displayed on screen.

Computers are digital; they represent data in a series of zeros and ones; they have no awareness of colour and the perception of colour. A 24-bit RGB value is represented in hex as #FF0000. We currently know this as red; the computer does not. It is possible for it to display this colour as green, blue or even pink unless it has been mapped to some reference representation correctly. This is where colour spaces and colour management come in.

The colour space allowing us to represent red in the previous example is an RGB colour space, specifically sRGB. As such there is no conflict between our representations and how it is displayed to the user. Colour management simply ensures that this representation is reproduced as closely as possible across all output devices for our digital image.

A common scenario highlighting the need for colour management is printing. While printing might not be the primary objective of some digitization projects the *potential* requirement should be considered. Printing uses the CMYK colour model as opposed to sRGB. The CMYK colour model is capable of representing a different subset of colours than sRGB; it has a different gamut. It is because of this difference that if you were to naïvely print an sRGB photo using a CMYK device the colours are likely to come out differently than expected, specifically extremes of red, green and blue. This difference needs to be managed so that the output looks as close to the original as possible. This is normally achieved using a colour profile that maps the differences between the two colour spaces.

Colour profiles are used to ensure the quality of reproduced colour across many output devices. While these potential uses cannot be second-guessed, the minimum requirement for most projects should be an input profile detailing the colour space of the device that was used to digitize the object. The preservation of appearance – colour being a part of that appearance – is crucial to many applications of digital images. Calibration, that is, normalizing the imaging equipment to provide a consistent representation of the analogue in digital form, is also required as part of the colour management process to ensure that imaging devices provide accurate and reliable results throughout the digitization process.

Archival masters vs. service copies

Archival masters vs. service copies – The images that come directly from the digitization process will form a group of archival master images. These images will be of the highest quality, of the largest file size and will be of a format that characterizes that requirement. It is highly unlikely that these images will be served directly to the end-user. It is important that the archival master sits within a digital repository where it will be preserved and the file migrated as required over time, should the present format start to become obsolete.

The maintenance of the master need not be an expensive process as it merely involves understanding the file formats the master images are stored as and the threat to the ability to read and use that format over time. Image formats such as TIFF (Tagged Image File Format) have proven to be robust and have lasted over time. This has proven to be a trend among other image formats as well. Workflows to achieve this can be set up relatively easily using modern computing techniques. The successful maintenance and control of archival masters will prevent additional costs in future to redigitize collections.

The service copy will be derived from this master. Delivering content digitally, over networked resources for example, requires different image types. While delivery of a master image might be possible this way, regular access to images warrants a smaller file size. To achieve this, a file format might be used, such as JPEG (Joint Photographic Experts Group) which compresses the image, potentially using lossy techniques. Lossy compression removes information perceived to be unimportant to the display of the image and often results in a reduction in image quality that cannot be recovered. While image quality is reduced, it results in a file size that is preferable for transfer across the internet without removing detail that researchers are interested in. Further, the same file might be used to create thumbnail images that can give users a preview on websites.

As will be discussed under the section about image specification in this chapter, the file formats available for selection for either archival masters or service copies might provide additional features from either of these versions of the image. Progressive transmission or progressive decoding of an image, for example, can allow a smaller, lower resolution version of an image to be displayed as it is transmitted to users. As more data arrives at the user's computer, the application displaying the image has more information to display a higher resolution image, getting progressively higher and higher. This is similar to someone showing a small version of an image, then a slightly larger one, and then a slightly larger one than that, until it is as large as it gets. Practically, this technique used in a file format can enhance the end-user experience by allowing the user to see a version of the image sooner, without having to wait for the entire file to be transmitted. As more features such as this are introduced into file formats it will become increasingly desirable to use archival masters for delivery, stored in newer, better formats. This has its advantages and disadvantages but certainly provides an elegant solution to reducing disk space requirements.

Post-processing

Once in possession of the digitized image it is possible to apply any post-processing technique required. While it is prudent to do this with an image other than the archival master, post-processing means images can be enhanced or even corrected should the digitization process not have produced a satisfactory result.

Image enhancement

There are many approaches to image enhancement. *Histogram equalization,* for example, increases the global contrast of a picture by distributing pixel intensities across the entire image. In some image manipulation programs the *curves tool* provides an alternative mechanism to modify contrast as well as colour and the brightness of an image; tweaking the curves is a sophisticated technique but can provide most of the basic image enhancement that might be needed in the post-processing stages.

Alternative post-processing techniques improve the dimensions and positioning of the image. First, *cropping* can be achieved very simply in the majority of image editing applications. Cropping allows users to remove a fixed region around the edges of an image. In many cases this might be to remove additional white space featuring around the image after scanning. In other cases it is used to cut the image down to strictly the relevant data; the page of a book, for example, might have its entire border removed by cropping, leaving just the text.

Second, *de-skew* can be used on images which have been scanned at an angle, or are crooked. If you are looking at the page of a book one might expect its sides to appear completely vertical. Scanning, however, might have been done at a slight angle so the page edges are slanted. The de-skew process corrects this by orienting the pixels in the scanned image so that it appears correctly. Again, this can be achieved with ease in the majority of image editing applications.

Compression

Storage requirements and reduction of the amount of space taken up by digital images has been mentioned previously. The storage of data does have a cost impact. As part of an approach to reducing storage costs, compression might be used.

Compression can depend on the selection of file format. A file format may or may not offer a compression mechanism and, if it does, the compression may be lossy or lossless. TIFF (Tagged Image File Format), for example, offers four techniques for compression on top of a zero compression configuration (Adobe, 1992).

Compression optimizes the disk space taken up by a digital file by taking advantage of redundancy found in digital information. An illustration of this redundancy might be a pixel-oriented run-length encoding technique that can be applied to bi-level images (Salomon, 2008). As an example, the first row of pixels in a 200 x 200 pixel image might be represented using 25 bytes, made up of 10 white pixels, 50 black pixels, 46 white pixels, 5 black, 4 white, 14 black, 6 white, 33 black, 32 white. Recording just the sequence of these pixels using integer values and using the assumption that all values beginning the sequence are white (outlined in the compression specification) we reduce this first row of pixels from 25 bytes to just 9 bytes (a byte per integer value).

More complicated data compression techniques exist but most work on a similar premise to represent the data, removing redundant information or perceivably redundant information. The difference between the former and latter techniques represents the difference between lossless and lossy compression. Lossless attempts to store information and represent it in a more efficient manner but using a technique that means that the format is the same decoded as it was before encoding. Lossy techniques remove information considered or perceived to be irrelevant to the representation meaning that the image is different decoded from the image before encoding.

The distinction between lossy and lossless is important, especially from an archival point of view, but keeping master copies of digitized images in a lossy format is not best practice. An additional note about lossy or lossless compression techniques is the existence of a term called 'visually lossless'. This represents a modern definition of lossy compression whereby the information thrown away as part of the compression process is considered to be unperceivable by the human eye. This term is slightly insidious and although one might not perceive differences immediately, on closer examination or after the application of image processing techniques it is likely that differences from the original image can be seen. This has an impact for scholarly research such as the palaeography example given earlier in the chapter.

Certain types of compression carry with it a performance impact. Where baseline performance figures are not available to understand this impact within a workflow or delivery mechanism, it may be necessary to conduct project-specific testing to find out the impact. Computationally expensive encoding and decoding of formats implementing wavelet transformation or fractal encoding could prove too expensive for viable use within a project or within certain phases of a project, such as serving an image stored using that compression technique to a consumer.

Image specification

In writing the image specification, one of the first elements you might think about is *file format*. File format encompasses everything that is found in a digital image. The choice of file format will dictate compression, use of colour management, bit-depth and metadata, among other requirements. File format may also provide desirable features such as progressive rendering or may have good web browser support for delivery and accessibility.

Some well known and popular formats that exist are TIFF, PNG (Portable Network Graphics), JPEG and formats that are less well known but are currently being investigated by the archival community, including JPEG2000 and JPEG XR (Joint Photographic Experts Group, 2000 and XR respectively).

It is important to review the specifications of a file format carefully to see if it matches requirements. Further, it is likely that more than one file format will be useful for your needs. For example, JPEG compression might not be suitable for archival masters but it might provide an excellent solution with relatively good image quality and smaller file sizes than TIFF as service copies for delivery over networks.

Some formats, however, might be useful as an archival master and some for delivery using special techniques such as progressive rendering. JPEG2000 might fit this purpose but support for the format is not widespread, which will be a consideration if accessibility is considered important to a project as end-users might not easily be able to find tools to render JPEG2000 images.

A specification may recommend multiple file formats, especially if the specification is to be given to external suppliers. The specification should be very clear about the type of object being scanned or photographed and the details for that digitization.

Image specifications should be as high as possible. One of the benefits of digitized objects is the manipulations and techniques that might be used on them and so, as previously mentioned, it is important to specify a requirement for images with the highest possible and highest achievable standards for our time. Once the specification has been outlined, *quality assurance* processes should be considered. It is important to make sure that processes, internal or external, are producing images of the standard that is expected.

The amount of metadata that can be stored about the analogue object is boundless. Suggested metadata to keep about the image includes the image specification – resolution, format, colour-depth, compression, etc. Detailing the type of compression used is important as it is impossible for a machine to tell if an image has been compressed using lossy techniques. The only mechanism to control this is good management of the digitized image and its associated metadata. We do not want to have to redigitize the analogue object unnecessarily so this might become a challenge as the image changes stewardship from generation to generation. The maintenance of digital images is made much easier over time by keeping good matadata.

Data such as this will form part of a provenance record that details the original scanning process, scanning device, and, amongst other things, when the image was first created, enhancements made to it, or, if applicable, when and how it has been migrated to another file format previously. A description of the analogue object including original dimensions, purpose and transcriptions of any text from the object can also be encoded as metadata.

While metadata can sit independently from the digital image it is preferable to associate it by writing it to the same file. Many image formats encode image data but also provide the facility to encode additional information about that image in the form of metadata. Some formats may be fairly prescriptive about how metadata is stored; however, others such as JPEG2000 offer the ability to encode raw, well formed XML (Extensible Markup Language) which allows you to store many different kinds of metadata. The type of metadata desired for storage may therefore have a bearing on choice of file format and thus software capable of processing, displaying and editing the metadata.

Metadata can be written in a wide variety of formats. We do not discuss the assortment of choices here; however, selecting standard formats such as RDF XML (Resource Description Framework) to encode metadata using established vocabularies such as Dublin Core or Digital Curators promotes the communication and the sharing of assets by using open, machine-readable file formats that provide interoperability across a myriad of potentially heterogeneous systems. This is essential for institutional and cross-institutional programmes such as resource discovery, a technology seeking to ensure that valuable information is found, retrieved and presented. DigiCULT (2004) presents a good summary on this technology in the context of heritage institutions.

Setting a standard

It is difficult to find a common standard within the field of digital image specifications. Part of the problem lies in the wide range of objects one is likely to digitize and the *raison d'être* of the institution doing the digitization work – different projects have different needs. It is possible, however, to look over the fence at what others are doing. Standards within institutions are appearing.

Guidelines from the likes of the Public Record Office Victoria (2010) or the California Digital Library (2009) can help digital curators. Organizations that support public sector bodies, such as JISC Digital Media (2010), provide further help on the subject of digitization and the entire digital workflow. Standards bodies such as the International Color Consortium (ICC) maintain guidance that covers digitization workflows and how their standard for colour management fits into imaging projects. This information can be found with ease using resources such as the internet.

The practical considerations of an image specification must also be examined. Increasing the amount of information in an image increases its file size. Using truecolor rather than greyscale increases the bit-depth and thus adds information contributing to the file size. File size will be impacted by a number of other decisions, including the choice of file format, compression and selected resolution – the greater the resolution the more data that is encoded by the image.

Beyond file size, we must consider the impact of the file formats we select. The use of TIFF for example means large file sizes but also a well supported, long lasting, robust file format – proven in many digitization workflows and still used to this day. Support and tools available to view and edit and migrate from TIFF are abundant. Choosing a modern format such as JPEG2000 might result in it being harder to find software and tools that fit into an institution's workflow, but this might be outweighed by the benefits of the format. Having said that, the format is also more complicated than TIFF and the processing (encoding/decoding) of it is much slower. The performance and delivery of the format are important considerations depending on the end-use.

De-facto standards exist. Formats and techniques which can be found across numerous institutions have the benefit of being proven to work. This should not prevent using novel or innovative approaches, however. A certain combination of settings will work best in a particular institution and in the absence of a specification that fits your purpose it is always possible to experiment with combinations of tools and settings to find what is best. Sharing the result of this testing and benchmarking will go a long way to helping other institutions and hopefully reveal common ground to help build something approximating a general standard in the long run.

Chapter summary

- Basic decisions relating to the image specification are: desired resolution, bit-depth/colour-depth and colour management.
- Image specifications depend on the intended use, options available and long-term preservation plans.
- The higher the image specification, the more server space the images will take up. This will have long-term implications for the host institution and must be considered at the outset.
- There should always be a high quality copy serving as an archival master image from which service copies can be made. Service copies can be manipulated to suit the desired presentation standards.
- Minimum post-processing should be completed on the archival master but conservative usage can enhance or correct images should the digitization process not produce a satisfactory result.
- Currently there are no standards for image specification. However, developing one's own standard and sharing it across numerous institutions will help to develop common ground and build towards a standard in the future.

Bibliography

Adobe (1992) *TIFF Revision 6.0 Final - June 3, 1992*,
    http://partners.adobe.com/public/developer/en/tiff/TIFF6.pdf.
California Digital Library (2009) *CDL Guidelines for Digital Images*,
    www.cdlib.org/services/dsc/tools/docs/cdl_gdi_v2.pdf.
DigiCULT (2004) *Resource Discovery Technologies for the Heritage Sector*,
    www.digicult.info/downloads/digicult_thematic_issue_6_lores.pdf.
JISC Digital Media (2010) *Advice on Still Images*,
    www.jiscdigitalmedia.ac.uk/stillimages.

The MathWorks (2010) *Image Types,*
    www.mathworks.com/access/helpdesk/help/techdoc/creating_plots/f2-
    10709.html.

Prescott, A. (2008) The Imaging of Historical Documents. In Greengrass, M. and
    Hughes, L. (eds), *The Virtual Representation of the Past*, Ashgate Publishing
    Limited.

Public Record Office Victoria (2010) *Digitisation: image requirements,*
    www.prov.vic.gov.au/publications/publns/1002s2.pdf.

Salomon, D. (2008) *A Concise Introduction to Data Compression*, Springer.

Twycross, M. (2008) Virtual Restoration and Manuscript Archaeology. In
    Greengrass, M. and Hughes, L. (eds), *The Virtual Representation of the Past*,
    Ashgate Publishing.

4

The process of selection

Introduction

Having addressed some of the fundamental issues at an institutional and technical level the next question to ask is 'what should we digitize?'. Astute decisions at the selection stage will build a robust programme of digitization projects that enhance the value of an institute's holdings, broaden audience engagement and make a genuine contribution to the welfare and knowledge of a collection. Implementing a good selection policy also helps to ensure that projects are logistically feasible and adequately resourced, while selection that lacks focus or is ill-informed can result in a rambling succession of projects where the overall costs ultimately outweigh the benefits.

A strategy for digitization

For most institutions it is not feasible to digitize their entire collection. Since 2004, commercial partners have invested an estimated £53 million in The National Archives UK's digitization programme, delivering more than 80 million images online, but this only represents 3–5% of the entire collection (Morley, 2009). Even for a collection of thousands rather than millions of items the costs and logistics of digitization can be prohibitive. A process of selection is therefore needed to identify suitable collections.

Once collections are selected for digitization these need to be prioritized so as to develop a digitization programme. Aims and priorities vary between institutions and the objectives of a digitization programme should be in keeping with institutional goals, be that to preserve national treasures, utilize local history sources for education or develop partnerships with academic bodies. It may be appropriate for a digitization programme to be accompanied by a digitization strategy to explicitly state the aims and objectives of digitization.

Examples of digitization strategies
Digitization for access: The National Archives UK

Project Motorway, the digitization strategy of The National Archives UK, aims to make 90% of the archive's most popular documents available online. This is in response to increased user expectations to find, use and learn from online resources. The National Archives UK achieves its aims with the help of grant funding sources for content that is mainly of specialist interest and through teaming up with commercial partners for content that is more popular, such as documents of interest to the family history market. In addition, the archive funds some smaller projects internally (Ahmon, 2009). The strategy is, on the one hand, very focused on popular content and, on the other, somewhat opportunistic by allowing commercial partners to digitize content known to be of interest to their market. In doing so it allows the archive not only to present its records online, but also to create a steady revenue stream as long as contents remain popular.

Digitization for preservation: Metamorfoze

Metamorfoze is the national programme for the conservation of Dutch printed and written heritage. It is financed by the Dutch Ministry of Education, Culture and Science and funds projects to preserve collections through the production of surrogates with the aim of making these accessible to users instead of originals. Since 2008, the focus of Metamorfoze has shifted from microfilm as a form of surrogacy to digitization. However, the Metamorfoze programme remains unique in its strategy to digitize collections on a large scale as a form of preservation. The stated aims of the programme are the prevention of decay, conversion of analogue information to digital information and preserving the original through optimal housing and storage (Metamorfoze, 2010). Its handbook, as published in 2008, details the collections qualifying for the programme and states which aspects make a collection significant enough for inclusion in the programme (Metamorfoze, 2008).

Digitization for education: JISC

JISC's mission is to inspire UK colleges and universities in the innovative use of information and communication technologies (ICT) in order to help maintain the UK's position as a global leader in education, research and institutional effectiveness. Its strategic objectives for the years 2010–12 include, amongst others, the provision of shared national resources and the improvement of quality of learning and teaching through digital technology (JISC, 2010a). The digitization strategy 'emphasises the creation of digital content that is relevant to particular areas of the curriculum or research interest, would not otherwise be funded, is at risk from being lost to the educational community, and contributes to creating a critical mass within a given area' (JISC, 2010b).

The principles and process of selection

The digitization of original materials is not needed if a microfilm surrogate is already available and can be digitized instead. If this is found to be the case then this option should be pursued in the first instance (see Chapter 2 'Before you digitize: resources, suppliers and surrogates'). The status of a collection in terms of ownership and copyright must be clarified because there may be legal reasons why a collection cannot be digitized and made available online. There may also be data sensitivity issues around the content of the collection, for example if documents contain medical records or other forms of personal information. If information is potentially sensitive then it is advisable to contact relevant groups to establish support for the digitization project.

Once these key issues are resolved then the criteria for selection can be distilled down to three core factors: content, demand and condition (UNESCO, 2002, 13–14). However, there are many aspects to each of these criteria. Much has been written on the subject of selection because it is such a fundamental element of a digitization programme. In particular, Hughes (2004, 31–53) and Hazen, Horrell and Merrill-Oldham (1998) provide a comprehensive overview of the issues. Since digitization takes place in the context of an institution's goals and priorities it is not surprising that there is great diversity in the approach to selection, as found by Ooghe and Moreels (2009). Their study also confirms how complex the procedure is but suggests some common ground to form a framework for more consistent decision-making across the heritage sector. Since selection criteria are covered in detail by other authors, we will focus here on the process itself and the role of the collection manager.

The proposal

An institution may have an unambiguous vision to digitize to improve access, or specifically to ensure preservation. In either case the process of selection can start by identifying the most popular collections on the one hand, and the most vulnerable collections on the other. However, this approach may not be sufficient for establishing a sustainable programme of digitization; in which case a much broader wish-list of potential projects is needed. These candidates can then be evaluated, selected or rejected, and then prioritized.

Some institutions invite members of the public to propose collections for digitization, for example, the National Archives of Australia (2010) invites nominations via its website. Others appeal to the research community, such as the British Library's (2010) Greek Manuscripts Digitisation Project which invites suggestions via its Medieval and Earlier Manuscripts blog. In other instances, an institution may be approached by a user group who have an interest in a specific collection. However, it is more likely that proposals for digitization projects will come from the institution's staff since they will have in-depth knowledge of the collections, as well as experience of which ones are significant and popular.

An alternative to inviting proposals is to establish a working group to proactively identify and propose potential collections for digitization. This group would need to have an overview of the aims of the digitization programme and the basic criteria that are required. They would therefore need to have expertise in a range of areas. Collections that were proposed via this route would still need to go through the same selection process as other proposals.

Selection procedure

A procedure for processing proposals should be in place so that the process is consistent and runs smoothly. A form or checklist can be useful as a way to construct a proposal that is focused on the relevant facts. At these early stages only basic information is needed (see Figure 4.1), but this may still require contributions from specialists including conservation staff. If a standard form

1 Name of proposer
2 Catalogue references of documents being proposed
3 Entire collection or part collection?
4 Brief description of content
5 Describe format (e.g. books, rolls, files)
6 Available in microform or originals only?
7 Why should the documents be digitized (consider popularity, enhanced access, preservation issues)
8 Any problems such as fragility or data sensitivity

Figure 4.1 *An example of a proposal form*

is used then this can include prompts to contact appropriate people. Compiling even the most basic information and drafting a proposal may seem time-consuming, but this really is a minimum requirement. Without all the relevant information an informed decision cannot be made.

The proposals process should include a named contact who can assist proposers if needed. There should be a timetable so that it is clear when the proposer can expect a verdict. The process should also be documented so that there is a record of the proposal and the decision.

The panel

As discussed in Chapter 2 'Before you digitize: resources, suppliers and surrogates' digitization projects require the involvement of staff with a range of skills and experience. Selection should ideally be carried out by a panel of staff so that proposals are considered from all angles and the views of different stakeholders are considered (Vogt-O'Connor, 2000). The composition of the panel will depend to some degree on the priorities of the organization. For example, if there is an emphasis on access it may be appropriate to have representatives from education and press departments. Since logistics play a large part in the feasibility of a project there could be someone from the in-house copying department and another from document delivery (who would also have a view on the popularity or otherwise of a collection). If copyright or data protection may be factors then there should be someone to advise on information policy or legal issues.

The collection manager undoubtedly has a role on the selection panel. They will need to report back on the physical nature of the collection and provide a view on how this will affect the collection's feasibility as a digitization project (see section below 'The impact of physical format and condition'). However, they will also have an interest in being informed of developments in the digitization programme because of the implications that this will have on resources. There may also be cases where the collection manager proposes collections that would benefit from digitization for preservation reasons.

Given the number of stakeholders who may have an interest in these projects, the panel could easily become an unwieldy committee, and so it is important when considering who to involve to strike a balance between being inclusive but decisive. The selection panel may consist of two or three individuals with other specialists attending only as necessary – for a smaller institution this may be the only option. One way to satisfy stakeholder groups that their views are being considered is to ensure that the details of which are scoped beforehand and included in the proposal document. Similarly, it may be appropriate for the proposer to attend if it would help to make their case, however, if the proposal form has enough information then this may not be necessary. The selection meeting should be minuted and the minutes can be circulated to all interested parties so that these people are informed without needing to attend the meetings.

Selection

The actual business of selection can consist of a round table discussion but this might not be feasible if there is a high volume of proposals to consider or if, for any reason, it is difficult to reach a consensus. Hughes (2004, 44–7) suggests developing a system for cost/benefit analysis in order to facilitate the assessment and selection process. While 'cost' and 'benefit' will vary between institutions, Hughes suggests which factors should be considered while acknowledging that this is still a highly subjective process. Cost and benefit can be presented in a decision matrix. Setting up and administering a decision matrix may seem cumbersome, but the result is a decision-making process that is transparent and thoroughly documented. This is particularly important where a project has been proposed and then postponed for future consideration – the matrix is simply reviewed and updated when the time comes to reconsider the proposal. A matrix will also ensure that projects are evaluated in a consistent way.

The matrix suggested by Lee (2000, 15–33) can be used to weed out proposals that fail to meet basic criteria and to categorize the remaining proposals according to how they meet the needs of access, preservation and institutional strategies. However, this model does not take account of potential difficulties in terms of practical and technical challenges. These challenges may be costly to overcome or may actually render a project unfeasible. An alternative matrix by Hazen, Horrell and Merrill-Oldham (1998), the Harvard decision-making matrix, offers an approach that takes account of feasibility as well as cost. However, as reported by Brancolini (2000), many of these issues cannot be answered with a straightforward 'yes' or 'no' and in practice the main value of the matrix is as a checklist of questions to form the foundation of a selection policy.

Due to the complexity of the selection process there is no 'one size fits all' model for selection. It is therefore down to the individual institution to consider its digitization strategy and then develop a selection policy accordingly. This will involve deciding on what level of detail is appropriate. A decision matrix can facilitate the decision-making process but will need to be developed in line with the selection policy of the institution. The decision to use a matrix will therefore depend on whether it will be a help or a hindrance. The selection process should aim to strike a balance between being agile and able to respond to local needs, and being accountable.

The impact of physical format and condition

The collection must be assessed so that the collection manager can comment on its suitability for digitization in terms of its physical format and condition. At the selection stage this assessment does not need to be a full survey and a spot check will suffice. Surveys result in a level of detail that is not needed at the selection stage. In any case, the amount of resources that surveys require will probably mean that it is not feasible to carry out a survey for every collection that is proposed for digitization.

Conducting an initial assessment

The information gleaned from spot checks may seem sparse and incomplete, but it serves as in initial indication of what the digitization project would entail were it to go ahead. If potential difficulties are identified at this stage then these can be taken into account during selection and, if the project is approved, it can be approached with more realistic expectations in terms of the resource implications, timescales and cost. Once the project is approved, a collection survey will provide comprehensive data to inform these plans. Spot checks are also an excellent way for the collection manager to gain an overview of an institution's digitization plans so that future projects, which may have a significant impact on conservation resources, may be anticipated.

Spot checks are best carried out by a conservator who can assess the condition of the documents and identify potential problems with handling and imaging. The key questions for the conservator to answer at this stage are whether or not the collection is in a fit state for digitization and, if so, whether there are any significant practical difficulties with digitization of the collection. However, the conservator should remember that the preservation of a collection in poor condition can benefit from digitization. Recommendations should state whether or not a collection survey is needed and, if advised that one takes place, how much time should be set aside for it. This means that a survey can be included in the project plan so that if the project goes ahead it does so on the basis of a realistic timescale. Collection surveys are discussed in Chapter 5 'Surveying collections'.

Even before the document checks are carried out there may be sources of information that the conservator can utilize.

- *Catalogue* – may contain information on physical format. The catalogue will also give an indication of age, which can be an indication of potential problems, for example, iron gall ink. With experience, it is possible to anticipate the document format based on the catalogue description. For example, correspondence is likely to be highly varied and may include seals; registers on the other hand can be very consistent unless they are collected from various different sources. The catalogue may also contain information on how a collection is arranged, useful if the document format has changed over time, for example, if earlier records were loose papers, while later ones are bound volumes.
- *Location* – document location may be an indicator of format if the institution has a dedicated store for, for example, photographic material or rolled maps.
- *Conservation database* – records of the conservation studio may show that items from a collection have been conserved in the past, and if so, how

many have been treated, why, and what treatment was carried out.
- *Institutional knowledge* – not to be underestimated; asking colleagues can uncover a wealth of information about the background to a particular collection. The previous use of a collection is often an insight into its present day condition.

In addition, an institution may have other data, for instance, records of loan requests, which may be relevant. Mining a variety of sources will help to piece together a picture of a collection's background. For example, if the conservator finds a few items with fire damage in a collection, this raises concerns that further items may be similarly affected – institutional knowledge may reveal the cause of the damage, which may suggest that it only affects a small number of items.

The assessment is carried out by looking at a handful of items selected at random from the collection. If many collections are to be assessed for digitization then it is useful to have a form or checklist to facilitate the documentation of the checks. The documentaion should include a thumbnail photograph of a typical item to serve as an aide-memoire. A spot check of one collection can be completed in half an hour.

What to look for
Variations within the collection

The question of how variable a collection is can often be answered simply by looking at the items on the racking. If items are all housed in boxes of varying dimensions then this suggests that the contents are also variable. If a collection is split between several locations then this can also indicate that it consists of different document formats, for example, rolled items may be stored separately from flat sheets, or conserved items may be stored separately from non-conserved items. When examining the contents of boxes, be alert to folded items because they will be larger when opened out. Folded items may also be found in bound volumes and can prove to be problematic to image because they are attached to other documents.

There is apparently endless diversity in some collections of original documents. Documents will sometimes consist of several different types of paper, variously coloured, with a combination of typed and handwritten text in different inks. Sometimes different materials may be present such as seals and photographic material, and there are also infinite variations in binding styles, fastenings and configurations of fastenings.

All of these variations contribute to the richness of a collection and if the appropriate processes and equipment are employed then it is usually possible to image any original document without causing damage and with minimal interference to the document format. However, the processes and equipment need careful consideration and the image capture process itself can be arduous and time-consuming resulting in higher costs. The conservator must therefore raise these issues at the outset so that the selection panel, and later the project team, understand that the image capture will not be entirely straightforward. If the project is to go ahead then a collection survey will quantify the variables so that the image capture operation can be planned appropriately.

Size and scale

The size of the documents that are proposed for digitization will determine the size of the required equipment and this in turn will have an impact on the space needed for the image capture operation. For some collections, for example large rolled maps, specialized equipment will be needed. Also, very heavy items, such as bindings with metal fixtures, may limit the choice of equipment as some book cradles have a weight limit. At the proposal stage, the choice of equipment will be some way off but raising any possible issues at this early stage will serve to manage the expectations of the potential project team. Scale, in terms of the quantity of material, is an important factor at the selection stage and must be considered alongside uniformity because a relatively small project consisting of diverse material can be more complex and challenging than a larger project that is consistent.

Format and medium

Considerations of format will include investigating whether a collection is already available on microfilm. If so, then enquiries should be made into the condition and quality of the film and whether or not the collection has been filmed in its entirety or only in part. Some document formats are easier to image than others, for example, unpacking bundles of folded papers is fiddly, slow work, but this can be an additional incentive in favour of digitization as the digital copy will provide access to documents that are otherwise not easily accessible. Similarly, some media are inherently unstable or vulnerable and in such cases special precautions may be necessary for their digitization, but these collections may also be good candidates for digitization in order to provide access while safeguarding the originals.

Condition

The conservator may come across damaged and deteriorated items during the spot checks, but even if items are in a good condition then the document format and the age of the collection will suggest the types of damage that are likely to be found. The conservation database, where available, will give an insight into what proportion of the collection has received treatment previously, and the nature of the damage. The conservator can then form a view on whether or not the collection would require extensive preparation before digitization. This may be the deciding factor if documents would require a great deal of work but are only moderately attractive in terms of content and use. However, vulnerable documents which are inherently unstable and have significant content may be good candidates for digitization to provide access while safeguarding the originals. Digitization can also be an excellent opportunity for improving the housing and storage of the documents.

Prioritization

If an institution is fortunate enough to have many collections that would benefit from digitization, and that can be digitized, then it will need to prioritize. Vogt-O'Connor (2000) suggests a scoring system to rank collections according to value, risk and use and also provides examples of how this system would work in practice. Each collection is scored on the three factors. The sum of these scores gives an overall score for each collection, by which they are ranked. For simplicity, each factor has equal weight and if some collections have the same score then specific details can be taken into account, such as usage figures.

In this system, a high risk collection is one that is in poor condition or is inherently unstable and so is therefore a strong candidate for preservation copying, for example a collection of cellulose nitrate films, or a collection of brittle papers. However, a collection which is in a state of deterioration may be a less attractive candidate for digitization if the poor condition renders items unfit for handling, or as requiring extensive preparation beforehand. The risk category therefore needs careful consideration because a collection in poor condition would not necessarily merit a high score.

Special collections

There may be collections of individual items within a collection that transcend the usual selection criteria and are digitized because they are the 'treasures' of the institution. Such special collections may be well known to the extent that they are very closely associated with a particular institution. The significance of the material may therefore outweigh the other factors of popularity (special collections may have highly restricted access) and condition (these collections may be in good condition having received the attention of conservators over many years).

If a special collection is being considered for digitization then it should go through the same selection process as other projects. However the weighting of the various criteria may need to shift. For example, the preservation benefits may be relatively small if the institution already has many measures in place to protect these valuable items, such as restricted access. The most significant gain from such a project would instead be the enhanced reputation of the institution and the opportunity for publicity and prestige. An institution's website serves as a shop window and having the treasures on display online will bring recognition and may attract new audiences.

Special collections can be presented simply as an online exhibition, which in itself can generate plenty of interest. Online access lends itself particularly well to documents with great visual appeal such as illustrated manuscripts and this can be enhanced with technology designed to simulate page turning, such as the Turning the Pages online gallery at the British Library website (www.bl.uk/onlinegallery/virtualbooks). However, presenting a special collection online is also an excellent opportunity to enhance its value by providing a rich array of interpretive material. For example, on the website of The National Archives UK, Focus on Domesday includes contextual information on the origins of the Domesday Book and 11th-century society in England, resources for teachers, as well as games and a quiz (www.nationalarchives.gov.uk/education/focuson/domesday).

If a special collection is to be digitized then this presents an excellent opportunity to address any issues surrounding the conservation and housing of items because it is probably rare for every individual item to be handled systematically. Likewise, the conservation of special collections can present an opportune moment to digitize them as part of an overall preservation strategy. Where special collections are concerned, the imaging and the conservation of the documents may go hand in hand. For example conservators at The National Library of Australia conserved and prepared over 170 artefacts and documents for display in the major exhibition *National Treasures from Australia's Great Libraries*. Each item was then digitized and presented in an online exhibition at the same time as the touring exhibition (Rozmus, 2006). The online exhibition remains accessible on the internet long after the touring exhibition has closed (http://nationaltreasures.nla.gov.au). In this example, digitization was carried out as part of a much wider project, not as a means to an end in itself.

Chapter summary

- Selection will depend on the goals and priorities of the institution's digitization strategy. Clarify from the outset if a collection is to be digitized from original or from microfilm. Also clarify any legal issues.
- The essential criteria for selection are content, use and condition, although there are many aspects to each of these and selection can be highly complex.
- The selection process can tap into the institutional knowledge of staff and the knowledge of users. The process should be open, inclusive and accountable. A decision matrix can help to keep the process consistent, but can be overly cumbersome if not well designed.
- The collection manager should comment on the physical format and condition of collections that are proposed for digitization and alert the panel to any significant problems.
- Special collections should also be selected using the same criteria and process, but there may be more of an emphasis on education and outreach.

Bibliography

Ahmon, J. (2009) Project Motorway: implementation of large-scale scanning projects. In Webster, J. and Reed, C. (eds) *Second Life for Collections: papers given at the National Preservation Office conference held 29 October 2007 at the British Library*, National Preservation Office.

Brancolini, K. R. (2000) Selecting Research Collections for Digitization: applying the Harvard model, *Library Trends*, **48** (4), 783–98, www.ideals.illinois.edu/bitstream/handle/2142/8310/librarytrendsv48i4j_opt.pdf? sequence=1.

British Library (2010) *Which Manuscripts Should we Digitise?* http://britishlibrary.typepad.co.uk/digitisedmanuscripts/2010/03/which-manuscripts-should-we-digitise.html.

Hazen, D., Horrell, J. and Merrill-Oldham, J. (1998) *Selecting Research Collections for Digitization, Council on Library and Information Resources*, www.clir.org/pubs/reports/hazen/pub74.html.

Hughes, L. (2004) *Digitizing Collections: strategic issues for the information manager*, Facet Publishing.

JISC (2010a) *Strategy 2010–2012*, www.jisc.ac.uk/aboutus/strategy/strategy1012.aspx.

JISC (2010b) *Digitisation*, www.jisc.ac.uk/whatwedo/topics/digitisation.aspx.

Lee, S. (2000) *Digital Imaging: a practical handbook*, Library Association Publishing.

Metamorfoze (2008) *Handboek Preservation Imaging, version 2.0*, Bureau Metamorfoze, Koninklijke Bibliotheek/Nationaal Archief.

Metamorfoze (2010) *Programma*, www.metamorfoze.nl/programma/index.html.

Morley, O. (2009) *Digitisation and Our Options for The National Archives Future Strategy*, The National Archives UK, internal presentation.

National Archives of Australia (2010) *Digitisation Program: making whole series available online*, www.naa.gov.au/services/digitisation-copying/program/index.aspx.

Ooghe, B. and Moreels, D. (2009) Analysing Selection for Digitisation: current practices and common incentives, *D-Lib Magazine*, **15** (9/10), www.dlib.org/dlib/september09/ooghe/09ooghe.html.

Rozmus, B. (2006) Digitising Australia's National Treasures, Gateways, **80**, www.nla.gov.au/pub/gateways/issues/80/story14.html.

UNESCO (2002) *Guidelines for Digitization Projects: for collections and holdings in the public domain, particularly those held by libraries and archives,* http://portal.unesco.org/en/ev.php-URL_ID=7315&URL_DO=DO_TOPIC&URL_SECTION=201.html.

Vogt-O'Connor, D. (2000) Selection of Materials for Scanning. In Sitts, M. (ed.), *Handbook for Digital Projects: a management tool for preservation and access: first edition,* Northeast Document Conservation Centre, www.nedcc.org/resources/digitalhandbook/iv.htm.

5

Surveying collections

Introduction

As explored in Chapter 4 'The process of selection', there are numerous physical aspects of a collection that will have a direct impact on the image capture operation. An initial spot check assessment will go some way towards identifying what some of the issues may be, but a more thorough investigation is needed in order to gain a comprehensive understanding of the physical nature of the collection. A collection survey is therefore an essential element of most digitization projects and should not be seen as an optional extra.

Why do a survey?

Many of the physical attributes of the documents will affect the choice of imaging equipment and so the sensible approach is to assess the documents before deciding on the most appropriate equipment. An obvious example is the need to ensure that the equipment is large enough to accommodate the documents. If the documents are different sizes then it may be economical to use different scanners for different sized documents – the survey could be used to identify what proportion of documents are larger or smaller, and also to establish the distribution of the different sizes. Chapter 6 'Equipment for image capture' examines what types of equipment are compatible with different document formats.

Variations within a collection are often a cause for concern for imaging operations. Historic documents can be incredibly diverse and variations mean that image capture can be slow and arduous if the camera operator has to frequently adjust settings to capture different sizes or colours of paper. Handling diverse material is also slower. When handling consistent sheets of the same size and weight, the operator becomes accustomed to the behaviour of the material and gets into a routine – with a result that the process becomes faster. Diverse material may require some decision-making because different documents may need to be processed differently; for example, some may have fastenings that need to be removed, or different documents may need to be handled differently. This will have the effect of slowing down the operation.

If the image capture is outsourced to a commercial supplier they will need to set competitive image capture rates so that the overall operation is financially viable. However, this may be unrealistic if it fails to take into account the time needed to safely pack and unpack the documents from their housings and handle them carefully during imaging. Whenever the operator encounters an unexpected difficulty then there is a delay while a solution is found. The impact of this is compounded for an imaging project that is scheduled to take months or even years. With constraints on time and finances it is essential to 'know your documents' so that these difficulties can be anticipated and expectations can be managed.

For the conservator the focus of a survey is likely to be the condition of the documents and the question of what work is needed to prepare items for image capture. This will also have a bearing on the planning of the image capture operation because the document preparation is usually one of the first stages of the process and so it is essential to include it in the project plan. Launching into a digitization project without considering document preparation will either result in unreadable images, or will cause delays if damaged documents are encountered and must be sent for conservation. There is also a risk to document welfare if damaged items are processed without being first stabilized by a conservator.

Conducting a survey
Initial spot check assessment

An initial spot check assessment, as described in Chapter 4 'The process of selection', usually provides sufficient information to be able to decide on the survey requirements. Three outcomes are possible from a spot check assessment:

1 No problems are found

It could be that all indications are that the collection is in good condition and format is consistent, so digitization should be straightforward. If this is the case then the conservator must make a decision, to the best of their knowledge, on whether or not to proceed with a survey. This decision should consider the amount of resource needed to conduct the survey and the potential benefits.

A cautious approach is recommended here. It is possible for a spot check to miss items that are problematic and if a survey is not carried out then these items may only be discovered during image capture. This need not have a critical impact on the imaging operation if only a few items are affected and only minimal intervention is required. However, a more serious problem, such as extensive mould damage, may have a more significant impact if there are many affected items that need to be removed from the production cycle for some time. If spot checks indicate the presence of any problem that may impede the imaging process then a survey would dispel doubts about the prevalence of the problem. A project should only proceed without a survey if the conservator is confident that the collection has no problems.

An additional factor to consider would be the question of who will be conducting the image capture operation. The staff at an in-house imaging facility may be familiar with historic documents and would therefore be sufficiently experienced to be able to deal with minor problems. At the other extreme, a commercial supplier may employ staff from a third-party employment agency who have no previous experience at all. Even if this is the case, it is possible to make use of document handling training and appropriate supervision to minimize risks to the documents.

2 Collection is unfit for digitization

As mentioned in Chapter 4 'The process of selection', an entire collection in fragile condition may be a candidate for preservation copying so as to improve access while reducing future handling of the documents. Examples would be collections that are fire damaged, mould damaged or that consist of very brittle paper. These documents may require extensive conservation work to stabilize them for imaging so if the resources for this work are not available then the project may be deemed unfeasible and be discarded altogether, or it may be postponed while other, more stable, collections are digitized.

If a very fragile collection is proposed for preservation copying, for example as part of a grant application, then a full survey may be undesirable because it will involve unpacking and handling fragile items. An alternative would be to conduct a pilot study to carry out conservation work on several representative items, an approach described by Lindsay (2003, 51). A pilot study leads to the development of a robust methodology for the treatment and an average treatment time per item can be calculated. This can be used to give a rough estimate of the time needed to prepare the entire collection, assuming that every item in the collection will require treatment. A pilot study is likely to be more time-consuming than a survey but pilot studies can replace surveys where the quantity of items in need of treatment is known because the collection is already well documented – either the whole collection requires treatment, or items in need of treatment have already been identified. Another benefit of a pilot is that it will result in a small sample of the collection being ready for imaging.

The spot check may indicate that only part of the collection is fragile, in which case one option would be to go ahead with the digitization but exclude unfit items from the image capture. In this case, a survey would be needed to establish how much of the collection is affected and to identify those items that are unfit. If a sampled survey indicates that only a small number are affected then unfit items can be filtered out during the imaging operation. Ways of approaching this are discussed in Chapter 8 'Preparation of damaged documents'.

Excluding unfit items would result in gaps in the digital surrogate but this may be acceptable for a vast collection where condition is simply one of several selection critera, as was the case for the Dutch Prints Online project (www.dutchprintonline.nl). This project focused on printed material from 1781 to 1800 in Dutch or French where the content is of historical, political, theological or literary interest. Items meeting these criteria were selected from the library collections of three Dutch institutions so if an item was considered to be too vulnerable to be imaged it was simply omitted and an alternative was selected instead (de Boer, 2010).

Alternatively it may be possible to source a replacement. Libraries may have more than one copy of an item in their collection and so can choose to digitize the copy that is in the best condition. Alternatively, there may be copies in other institutions that can be used to fill gaps in the digital surrogate.

For example, when digitizing its newspaper collection, the Dutch National Library was able to complete incomplete titles via loans from other institutions (de Boer, 2010). For an archival collection that consists of unique material, it may be possible to source associated documents to compensate for gaps in the surrogate, since it is unlikely that a like-for-like replacement exists.

3 Survey needed

For the majority of collections this third scenario is the most likely. In this case observations from the initial spot check assessment indicate that some documents will have problems that will need to be addressed prior to imaging. A survey is therefore needed in order to quantify the extent of the issues and estimate the resources that will be needed to address them. It is essential that the survey is carried out as soon as it is clear that a project is going ahead. The planning stage of the digitization project must therefore allow time for the survey and analysis of results because the survey will provide information that can have a crucial impact on the imaging operation and hence the timescale for the whole digitization project.

Planning a collection survey

Conservation professionals are familiar with collection surveys for assessing condition and conservation requirements. The basic principles for surveying a collection for digitization are the same as those for surveying any collection's condition. These principles are outlined by Keene (1996, 136–71). In order to be effective, a survey should always be designed to answer key questions, so as to avoid wasting time by accumulating superfluous data.

How long will it take?

A collection survey need not be a huge drain on resources and a collection consisting of a few hundred items can easily be assessed within two weeks. The time taken to assess an item will depend on its format and condition. An experienced conservator can assess the condition of a bound volume in a matter of minutes, so could potentially assess at least 50 items in one day.

Damaged items would need to be looked at more carefully, but a rate of 30 bound volumes a day is still achievable. Boxes of loose papers would take much longer, as would items with intricate housings such as folded bundles of papers.

The resources needed to carry out a survey can be estimated based on the time taken to carry out the spot check assessment. Teams of two or three working together can get the job done quicker and may be essential, for instance when handling heavy or especially large items. However, it has been found that assessment of condition can be highly subjective (Taylor and Stevenson, 1999) so if a survey is to be carried out by a team then an initial briefing meeting is needed to ensure that the criteria are understood by all and that a consistent approach is maintained.

Who will do the assessment?

The survey should be carried out by a conservator because the assessment involves:

- identifying damage and potential problems such as fastenings
- understanding how these issues will affect the imaging process
- knowing what steps are needed to address any issues
- estimating how long preparation of the documents will take.

An understanding of different materials and their deterioration, as well as binding structures and the ability to distinguish between original material and previous repairs, will all play a part.

Ideally, the survey should be done by the same conservator who will be carrying out the preparation of the collection in question, and preferably someone who has carried out preparation for image capture before. This is the best way to ensure accurate time estimates. However, this is often not possible if the work is to be done by temporary project conservators or because of the particular timescale involved – the planning stage of a large-scale digitization project can take a year or more.

Survey method

The survey cannot start until a complete list of documents to be digitized is available. It is dispiriting to carry out a survey only to find that the list was incomplete or has since been changed. It is important to clarify from the outset what is considered to be an 'item' and to maintain this consistently throughout the assessment. For example, in the context of an archive, an orderable unit could be a single volume or a single bundle of papers, or it may consist of a box containing several books. One orderable unit could even consist of several boxes, each containing a mixture of material. The simplest way to establish the basic unit for the survey would be to treat each unique catalogue reference as an item. This means that each item that is assessed can be easily identified, but it may also mean that assessing some items will involve examining a large quantity of material.

Logistically the most efficient and effective method may be for the conservator to enter the storage areas and conduct the assessments *in situ*, pulling items off the shelves as necessary. This means that not only do documents not need to be transferred to the conservation studio, but also that items remain available to readers. However, this approach can be complicated if a collection is stored in more than one location or if a project consists of items from several different collections with many different locations, including off-site storage facilities. It may therefore be more practical to temporarily relocate items so that everything is in one place. A dedicated workspace could be set up for surveys, particularly if surveying more challenging items such as large rolled maps.

Results should be recorded on a survey form, which can simply be a series of tick boxes. Alternatively the results can be entered directly into a database on a laptop or other portable device. The advantage of using paper forms is not only the foolproof nature of the medium, but also maintaining a live electronic database can be logistically difficult if several people are working on the same survey in different locations. The disadvantage is that the data needs to be typed into a database to be analysed. The database should be as simple as possible for ease and speed of data entry and analysis. A Microsoft Excel spreadsheet is perfectly adequate for a collection survey. See Table 5.1 for an example. When carrying out the survey, it is essential to make an entry onto the database for every item that is assessed even if the item is ready to image and no problems are noted. If only problematic items are recorded then the resulting statistics will be invalid as they will give a distorted picture of the condition of the collection.

Table 5.1 *Example of a survey form*									
Reference	Format	Loose inserts	Pasted inserts	Pins	Paper repair	Mould	Separation	Rehousing	Code
T 38/310	Pamphlets	N	Y	Y	N	Y	N	Y	4
T 38/311	Loose papers	Y	Y	N	Y	Y	Y	Y	4
T 38/312	Pamphlets	N	N	N	N	Y	Y	Y	3
T 38/313	Pamphlets	N	N	Y	Y	N	N	N	1
T 38/314	Pamphlets	N	Y	Y	N	N	N	N	0
T 38/315	Loose papers	Y	Y	N	Y	N	N	Y	2
T 38/316	Pamphlets	Y	Y	N	N	N	N	N	0

To sample or not to sample?

A full survey where every item is assessed will give a complete picture of the nature of a collection. It will ensure identification of every item in need of preparation and provide a comprehensive estimate of the time needed to prepare the collection for image capture. However, while feasible in cases of small collections, consisting of up to a few hundred items, conducting a full survey of anything larger can be a daunting prospect.

For larger collections it is possible to gather the necessary information by assessing a representative sample. Sampling not only saves time but also the quantity of resulting data is more manageable. It may be preferable to assess a sample when applying for grant funding because this will be quicker than a full survey while still providing reliable data. There are also practical reasons why a sampled survey may be preferable since it is more feasible for one person to complete the survey, resulting in more consistent results. Also, with fewer items to assess, the conservator can stay focused and can examine each item with more care and in greater detail.

The main disadvantage of assessing a sample is that the results do not give the comprehensive picture that a full survey would give. The survey may indicate that 100 items in a collection require repair, but it will not tell the conservator which 100 items. This is not a reflection on the accuracy of the results – if the sampling method is statistically sound then the resulting estimates are valid for the whole collection. However, at some point a second step is needed to assess the remainder of the collection. When deciding whether or not to sample, it is therefore important to consider the resources available to conduct the survey and the timescale involved.

Sampling methodology

It is important to sample enough items so that the survey results are statistically valid. The method for selecting those items is equally important. The conservator must not be tempted to select items for assessment because they look particularly vulnerable or simply because they look interesting. Sampling methodology used for consumer surveys and polls is derived from probability theory and statistical theory and the same methods can be applied to the surveying of collections.

Sample size

Sampling is simple to execute once a few basic principles are understood. It is easy to assume that assessing a given percentage of a collection (such as 15%) will always give a representative sample. However this is not the case. Sample size is relative to several factors.

- *Population size.* This is the number of items in the collection. Typically an item would be an orderable unit with a unique catalogue reference.
- *Confidence interval.* Also called margin of error, this is the desired accuracy of the results. A confidence interval of 5% is enough for collection surveys and means that results should be regarded with an accuracy of plus or minus 5%. A smaller confidence interval requires a larger sample size.
- *Confidence level.* This is the degree of confidence that the results are within the desired confidence interval. A confidence level of 95% is sufficient for a collection survey. A greater confidence level requires a larger sample size.

Once these factors are defined, mathematical formulae are used to calculate the required sample size. There are now numerous websites with sample size calculators that do this (for example, www.raosoft.com/samplesize). Alternatively Table 5.2 can be used as a guide to determine sample sizes that will give 95% confidence that results are accurate with a margin of error of plus or minus 5%.

Table 5.2 Sample sizes for given population sizes (confidence level 95%, confidence interval 5%)	
Population size	Sample size
500	218
1000	278
1500	306
2000	323
2500	334
3000	341
4000	351
5000	357
6000	362
7500	366
10,000	370
25,000	379
50,000	382

As seen in Table 5.2, the larger the population, the larger the sample size, but beyond a population of 6000 the sample size increases very little – so even a population of 50,000 requires a sample size of only 382. For a population of millions the required sample size does not go beyond 385 so selecting a sample of this number of items will always give results of sufficient accuracy, although for smaller collections a smaller sample will do.

Stratified sampling

For a more complex project consisting of several diverse collections, or a large collection that is made up of diverse sub-groups, a larger sample size is needed. The approach here is called stratified sampling and is appropriate if there is reason to believe that inconsistencies exist across the different groups within the project. For example, if a project includes several different collections then each collection should be spot checked. Supposing the spot checks reveal that, while the majority of collections are loose papers, there are a couple of small collections consisting of parchment bundles. If the project involves 5000 items then a sample of only 357 may miss the (two) parchment collections altogether.

One approach would be to carry out a full survey so that every item is assessed, or to look at a very large sample (such as alternate items). However both of these approaches will involve an unnecessarily large amount of data gathering. Statistically valid results can be obtained with considerably less work by adopting stratified sampling. This involves sampling each group separately. The results for each group would also be analysed separately but can then be aggregated for the survey report. Stratified sampling is therefore suitable for a very large project which consists of defined groups where the spot checks of these groups have indicated that the groups vary significantly.

Selecting the sample

There are two simple methods for selecting items for assessment. Both are valid and the choice between the two depends on the collection itself.

Random sampling

The sample can be selected at random from the catalogue listings. This is greatly facilitated if the catalogue is available online. A function in software such as Excel can be used to generate a list of random numbers which can be used to select catalogue entries, for example, by document reference. The list of random numbers can also be used to identify physical items *in situ*, for example, the third, twelfth and twenty-third items on the shelves. With random sampling, each item in the collection has an equal probability of being picked.

Systematic sampling

This method involves selecting one item at random and then subsequent items at regular intervals. The size of the intervals will depend on the sample size and the overall size of the collection; for example, according to the table above, a collection of 1500 items requires a sample size of 306 items, which is approximately every fifth item. This approach will work with catalogue listings but can also be used to sample a collection *in situ*, for example by selecting every fifth item on the shelves. It can therefore be used if the catalogue is not online or is incomplete. However, systematic sampling *in situ* is not suitable if the collection is in some way arranged systematically, for example if oversized items are stored on the bottom shelf, because then there is a risk that the resulting sample would be biased.

What to record

One of the main aims of the survey is to estimate the resources needed to prepare documents for imaging and so the first question is whether or not the item requires preparation. Even if the condition of the item is fine then there will still be basic information to record that will help to build a picture of the nature of the documents. Since collections vary widely it may be necessary to tailor the survey form for different projects – the spot checks should give an indication of what questions need to be answered.

Once the survey is underway, the form may need to be adjusted if a previously noted issue turns out to be insignificant, or, conversely, if a new issue crops up. A comments section is helpful for noting the details of any anomalies that are found, although qualitative data in the form of free text comments can be difficult to analyse. Comments will be easier to analyse if they use consistent terms and phrases. Some conservation studios already have an established vocabulary, but in general it is wise to keep entries in the comments field to a minimum. Before adding comments during a survey it is worth considering if the additional information is really necessary and, if so, what the information would be used for.

Condition

If the item is not stable enough to be imaged and requires preparation then there are two further questions to be answered: how long will the preparation take and what treatment is needed? The first question can be an estimated time or can be in the form of a damage code (see Table 5.3). See Table 8.2 in Chapter 8 'Preparation of damaged documents' for more detail on what conservation work can realistically be carried out in these timescales.

Using a code simplifies the data entry and provides some contingency –

Table 5.3 *Examples of damage codes*	
Damage code	**Estimated preparation time**
Code 0	no preparation needed
Code 1	up to 30 minutes needed
Code 2	up to one hour needed
Code 3	up to three hours needed
Code 4	up to six hours needed

provided the conservator rounds up their estimate. Using a damage code system can also give a more consistent assessment where the survey is carried out by a team, since the codes are arranged in ranges of time and the conservator is only required to provide an actual time estimate if the preparation is estimated to take longer than six hours.

Recording further details about the condition of each item should be restricted to aspects that will have an impact on the handling and processing of the document. If the type of damage is fairly consistent then it might not be necessary to record this information and the time estimate will be an indication of the quantity and extent of the damage. However, some specific types of damage are worth noting because they will have a bearing on the imaging.

Brittle or burnt paper

The decision to treat brittle paper should take into account the scale of the problem and other attributes of the document. Regardless of whether or not it is feasible to treat the brittle paper, it is likely to have an impact on the speed of image capture because of the extra care needed to handle the items and the time needed to clean debris from the scanning bed.

Damaged bindings

A damaged case binding may be easier to image than an intact binding if the sewing is loose and the case detached. However, image capture may be slower if the item needs to be unpacked from wrappings or ties, and a damaged binding may shed material when it is handled because loose and fragmentary materials can easily become detached (see Figure 5.1).

Figure 5.1 *Damaged bindings can be digitized but may shed material when handled*

Cockling or warping

Documents that are severely cockled or warped may be problematic if imaging equipment has a very narrow depth of field. This can result in parts of the image being out of focus because areas of the document were either too far from or too near to the imaging device. This can be a problem for both paper and parchment items.

Inappropriate or damaged housing

Documents may be sewn or otherwise attached into a housing that is problematic because it is difficult to open or has become damaged. This can result in damage to the document during transport and handling. A housing can cause difficulties during imaging if it is not compatible with imaging equipment. This could be because it does not fit on a scanner, it is too bulky, or because the verso of a document cannot be imaged easily (see Figure 5.2). Sometimes a particular housing can cause problems simply because it is difficult and time consuming to unpack and repack the documents. Original historic housings such as wrappings and ties can be complicated and tricky to remove.

Figure 5.2 *These parchment documents have been sewn into a housing, making it difficult to image the verso of each one*

If documents have been encapsulated in polyester sleeves, this protects and supports the documents when they are handled. However, the glossy plastic can cause reflections with some equipment that will interfere with the digital image and so if documents are permanently housed in sleeves then this should be noted.

Previous repairs

Most paper conservators are familiar with the sight of aged repair work which has failed due to heavy usage, or has deteriorated due to the use of inappropriate repair materials. Sometimes repairs were carried out by the document's previous owner using whatever office materials were to hand, such as adhesive tape, gummed labels or even fragments of other documents. Poor repairs can cause cockling and distortion of the paper that, in the worst case scenario, can lead to stresses in the document which results in fresh tears when the document is handled. Sometimes a repair is applied on top of text thus obscuring it completely (see Figure 5.3). Both the repair material and the adhesive may deteriorate over time and this can result in severe

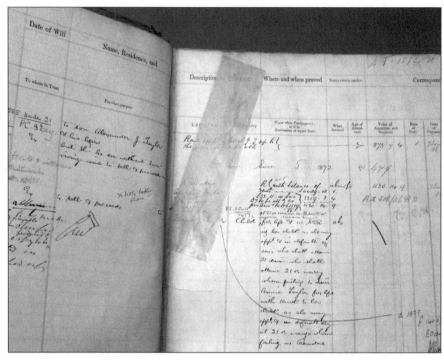

Figure 5.3 *A previous repair may need to be removed if it obscures text*

discolouration of the document (in the case of adhesive tape) and, ultimately, failure of the repair itself.

If previous repairs are identified as a significant problem in a collection then it would be advisable for a conservator to investigate further so as to get a better idea of the nature of the repairs and whether or not they will respond to treatment. In some situations, removal of a repair cannot be carried out without causing damage to the original document, or it may be the case that removal is too difficult and time-consuming to be feasible within the timescales involved. In addition, a repair is part of the history of the document so there might be good reasons not to remove it.

Ink corrosion

Historic documents will often suffer from see-through, where the writing on the verso has burnt through the paper due to ink corrosion (see Figure 5.4).

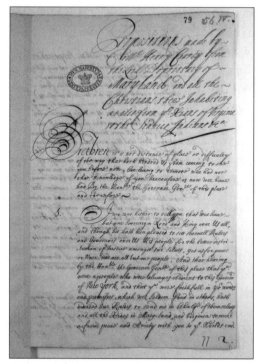

Figure 5.4 *Ink corrosion can affect the legibility of the text*

This effect cannot be corrected by conservation treatment but should be noted as it will affect the readability of the image.

Quantity

The quantity of items in a collection may seem like a straightforward question that can be answered by the institution's catalogue. However, since a single catalogue entry may refer to a box containing several items and an item can itself consist of several parts, a survey may be the best way to estimate the total quantity. Furthermore, the scope of a digitization project is usually concerned with the number of images to be captured, and so it is not sufficient to estimate the number of items.

The only way to estimate the total number of images in a project is to count the number of images in a selection of documents and extrapolate to estimate the number of images in the whole collection. The process is considerably easier if documents are already foliated. Since the number of images is so critical to establishing the scope of a digitization project this image counting may be one of the first things to be done, and so may be carried out separately from the collection survey. In that case the role of the survey would be to identify any anomalies.

Quantifying the number of images is complicated by several questions.

- Will covers be imaged?
- Will the verso side be imaged if it is blank?
- What if half a book is blank?

Imaging blank documents may seem like a waste of resources but if the aim is to create a digital surrogate then the documents should be imaged in their entirety. Imaging the blank verso of a sheet of paper will also satisfy the user that they have seen the whole document, and that nothing is missing. When handling the original document most users would probably turn it over to see the back, and so users of the digital surrogate should be given the same opportunity. However, if items are very consistent, for example certificates or standard forms each with a blank verso, then imaging the reverse would be unnecessary. The consistency of the documents and the context of use will determine whether or not it is appropriate to image blank sheets.

Size and weight

The most obvious impact of the physical size of a document is that the imaging equipment must be able to accommodate it. A document must be fully supported when it is imaged without hanging over the edge of the scanning bed or work surface. This means that the overall dimensions of a bound volume when open and lying flat should be considered. Dimensions may also vary within a document, for example sheets of different sizes may be housed in a single file or bound into a volume. Some of these sheets may be folded so that they are much larger than expected when unfolded to their full extent (see Figure 5.5).

Figure 5.5 *A bound volume may include folded sheets*

If a folded or rolled item is larger than the scanning bed then it may be possible to image it in sections with the remainder of the document folded or rolled to one side; for example, a parchment roll could be imaged one membrane at a time with the remainder of the roll held in place on both sides by weights. However, this may require a considerable amount of time-consuming manipulation and it should always be done with care so as to avoid causing damage or introducing creases.

Sometimes the thickness of an item should be noted because some equipment cannot accommodate very thick documents. For example, if an overhead scanner has limited depth of field then parts of a document, such as the first few pages of a thick bound volume, may be out of focus because they are too near to the imaging device. Equipment may also have physical limitations, for example some scanners have a fixed glass plate with limited space between the plate and the scanning bed. Typically, a thickness of more than 10 cm may cause difficulties.

The weight of the document may also be an issue; for example, scanners that have a hydraulic scanning bed will have a weight limit. Bindings can be extremely heavy if they have metal runners or fasteners, or bound volumes may be heavy simply due their enormous size. It is unlikely that the weight of each item needs to be recorded but if one person has difficulty lifting an item on their own it can be considered to be a heavy item and should be noted.

When recording dimensions it is usually not necessary to measure documents individually. Sizes can be recorded using the standard international paper sizes (A series) since scanning equipment is usually built to accommodate documents according to these standard sizes. A quick and easy method is to keep templates of A3 and A2 sizes to hand so as to quickly check to see if the document can be accommodated on an A3 or A2 sized scanning bed. Bear in mind that the scanning bed on a scanner is likely to be slightly oversized and so a slightly larger document could be safely supported, although the scanner may not capture the image all the way to the edge of the document.

Material and format

The material and format of the documents will have a bearing on the processing and handling during the scanning. Materials and formats likely to be encountered are listed in Table 5.4, along with potential issues.

Table 5.4 *Document formats and their impact on image capture*

Format	Impact on image capture
Loose paper	Often suffers from edge damage caused by handling.
	Likely to contain variations in size, weight and quality.
	Likely to contain various fastenings such as staples and paperclips.
	Care must be taken to maintain correct sequence and arrangement.
Folded loose paper	Can be tricky to unfold individual items – careful handling needed.
	Documents will not lie flat.
	Paper may be weak and vulnerable along edges of creases.
Bundles of folded papers (see Figure 5.6)	Same issues as with folded loose paper; in addition:
	Fiddly to untie and re-tie bundles.
	Care must be taken to keep associated documents together and to maintain sequence.
Paper files (see Figure 5.7)	Likely to contain many variations in size, weight and quality.
	Likely to contain various fastenings such as staples and paperclips.
Bound papers (see Figure 5.8)	May contain many variations in size, weight and quality.
	May contain folded items.
	Bindings may restrict opening.
Books, e.g. registers (see Figure 5.9)	A register or index may contain many blank pages.
Printed books	Printed publications may have tight bindings, making opening difficult.
	Margins in the gutter might be tight, requiring software to correct for curvature.
Small paper rolls	Document will not lie flat.
	Items must be unrolled to assess dimensions.
Parchment membranes	Ink is vulnerable to loss.
	Document will not lie flat.
Folded parchment	May need to be unfolded by a conservator before imaging.
Seals	Should not be placed under a glass plate due to the risk of breakage.
Photographic material	Specific imaging accessories are needed to image transparent photographic materials such as negatives.
	Photographic material is particularly vulnerable to inappropriate handling.
Maps and works of art	Large sheet material requires careful handling.
	Works of art may have a friable media.

Figure 5.6 *Bundles of folded papers*

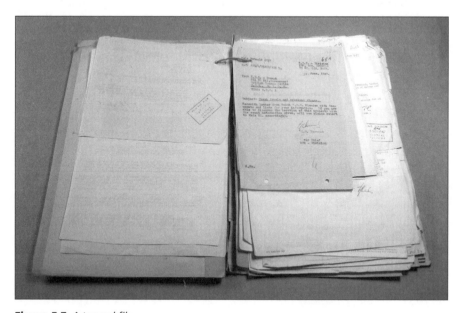

Figure 5.7 *A tagged file*

Figure 5.8 *Loose papers that have been made into a bound volume*

In addition to the physical format of items, there are other attributes that may be relevant to a project.

- Are documents typed or handwritten? Handwritten manuscripts are generally resistant to OCR.
- Standard forms can be easier to transcribe using a template to locate specific fields.
- Entries in a book may continue across a double-page spread. This should be captured in a single image, or, if captured in two images, the metadata should marry the two.

When designing the survey it is therefore helpful to be fully informed about the project brief and the content of the records as this may have a bearing on how the documents are to be processed.

Fastenings

There are a huge variety of ways in which loose documents can be fastened.

Unfortunately fastenings can restrict the opening of a document and imaging a document with a fastening in place can risk causing damage. This topic is covered in Chapter 7 'Preparation of document formats and fastenings'. When recording fastenings, it is necessary not only to make mention of whether documents have been fastened together but also the nature of any such fastening (stapling, tag-use, and so forth). In addition, it may be relevant to make a note if the arrangement of the fastenings is highly variable; for example, a document may be stapled along the spine or at the top or in a corner.

Inserts

Archival documents are inevitably created by people who find inventive ways to record information. Even standard forms will be annotated with inserts fastened in various arrangements and with the most resourceful of means. An insert may be glued on top of text in which case a decision will be needed on whether or not to remove it (see Figure 5.9). Elsewhere, an insert may restrict the opening of a document. Where an insert is smaller than the sheet it is attached to, the digital image must be cropped after imaging. An

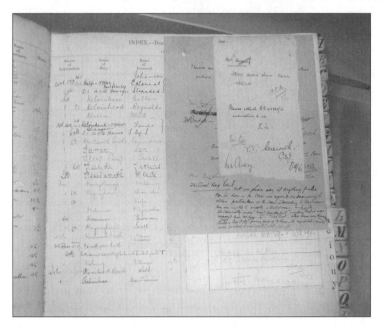

Figure 5.9 *Inserts pasted into an index*

alternative method is to insert a blank sheet behind the insert at the time of imaging so as to mask off the background.

Tight bindings

Some sewing methods and styles of binding can severely restrict the opening of the volume so that the volume will not lie flat and text is distorted by severe curvature at the gutter (see Figure 5.10). This is often a problem where stab sewing or over-sewing has been used to bind loose paper together. Sometimes if the text continues right to the edge of the sheet it might be lost in the sewing altogether. The issues surrounding disbinding bound volumes are discussed in Chapter 7 'Preparation of document formats and fastenings'.

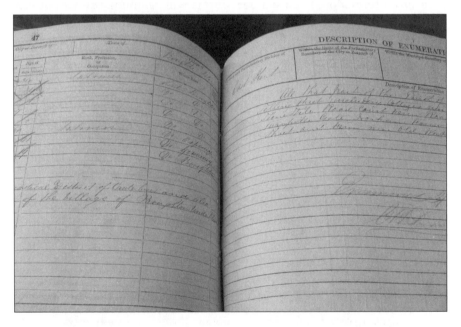

Figure 5.10 *Example of a tight binding that results in curvature at the spine edge*

Show through

Another issue is the use of very lightweight paper so that text on the sheet beneath is visible and can interfere with the image (see Figure 5.11). This can be addressed by the use of a blank backing sheet inserted behind the thin

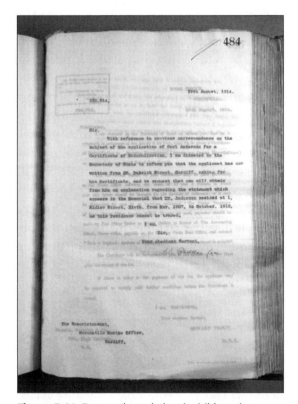

Figure 5.11 *Text on sheets below is visible owing*
to the lightweight nature of the paper

document at the time of imaging to obscure the document beneath. As such, it does not represent a problem, but will inevitably slow down the rate of image capture.

Anomalies

Sampling a collection might not identify rare anomalies since, by definition, an anomaly is out of the ordinary and not a common occurrence. However, anomalies may be found in full surveys and are worth noting so that they can be addressed, thereby avoiding nasty surprises during imaging. Unusual items such as framed photos, objects, an ornate binding or decorative original housing can be a delightful find and can add a new dimension to a digitization project.

Analysing data and making recommendations

The simplest way to present the figures is to state what proportion of the collection is ready to scan and what proportion requires some preparation work along with an estimate of how long this work would take. This can be presented in terms of an average treatment time per item, a useful concept as it is easily grasped. When calculating the time needed to prepare a collection for imaging, the figures are based on estimates so it is sensible to round up the figures. Quoting a figure to the nearest five minutes gives an inappropriate impression of accuracy to what is only an estimate. It would also be wise to add a contingency. If a sampled survey has been carried out then the amount of contingency can be based on the confidence interval used to calculate the sample size; for example, if a confidence interval of 5% was used then add a contingency of 5%. When estimating time based on a sampled survey it is important to include an estimate of the time needed to assess the rest of the collection.

Recommendations on scanning equipment may be irrelevant if imaging is to be done using in-house facilities. However, the survey may have highlighted specific issues to be considered at the planning stage so that they are taken into account when planning the workflow. For example, the document processing may have to include a step to remove staples. Recommendations for a digitization project may therefore look something like this.

- Description of the collection
  - quantity of items
  - format
  - size
  - anomalies.
- Recommendations for equipment and processing
  - specific issues that will have an impact on the imaging operation.
- Document condition
  - what proportion are ready to image
  - what work is needed to prepare documents for imaging
  - what resources are required to prepare documents.

The last section on document preparation should clarify the implications for the project. For example: recruitment of a project conservator, the required lead-in time for purchase of materials and preparation of documents. The recommendations should also suggest how to incorporate preparation work into the workflow of the imaging operation. This is dependent on a number of factors and is discussed further in Chapter 7 'Preparation of document formats and fastenings' and Chapter 8 'Preparation of damaged documents'.

Chapter summary

- For most digitization projects, a collection survey is an essential part of the planning process because it is imperative to know your documents.
- A survey might not be needed if the spot check indicates that there are no issues with format or condition, or if the entire collection will need preparation, suggesting that a pilot study would be more useful.
- A survey of a few hundred items can be completed in a couple of weeks, but the format and condition of items will affect the time taken to complete the survey. The survey team must include a conservator.
- If the project consists of more than a few hundred items then it is statistically valid to survey a sample instead of assessing every individual item. However, if assessing a sample then at some point the rest of the collection will need to be assessed.
- The survey data can be collected on a simple form. Only relevant data should be collected so the survey should be designed to suit the project.
- When analysing the data, be sure to add in contingency and to round up the figures. Recommendations should include advice on choice of equipment, the amount of document preparation needed and how the preparation should be incorporated into the imaging operation.

Bibliography

de Boer, T. (2010) personal communication.

Keene, S. (1996) *Managing Conservation in Museums*, Butterworth-Heinemann.

Lindsay, H. (2003) Preservation Microfilming and Digitization at London Metropolitan Archives: surveying and conservation preparation prior to image capture, *The Paper Conservator*, **27**, 47–56.

Taylor, J. and Stevenson, S. (1999) Investigating Subjectivity within Collection Condition Surveys, *Museum Management and Curatorship*, **18** (1), 19–42.

6

Equipment for image capture

Introduction

As seen in Chapter 5 'Surveying Collections', the physical nature of the documents can be highly diverse. These physical attributes will have a bearing on the choice of equipment because, needless to say, the equipment should not only be capable of capturing images of the required specification, but should do so without undue risk to the documents. There is a bewildering array of scanning products on the market with different capabilities and features, and different projects will have different requirements. Some equipment is designed for very specific applications and so would be perfect for a particular project but not suitable in the long term for scanning any other document format. On the other hand, a more flexible set-up can be used over the course of several different projects but may require some technical expertise to get the best results each time.

Choosing equipment for image capture is a common feature of all digitization projects and so there is an abundance of literature on the subject; see 'Further Reading' for details. This chapter will focus on the requirements of the original documents and the suitability of different types of equipment for different documents.

Risks during imaging

It is possible to image most documents safely and successfully if they are handled in an appropriate way using suitable equipment. However, digitization does involve some risks, the greatest of which is the risk of physical damage from handling.

Physical damage

In general, image capture involves handling that is far more intensive than the handling that a document will receive in an institution's reading room. Not only is there time pressure but also each sheet must be handled in such a way that every part of the page is exposed to the scanning device. This in itself can be hazardous for a fragile document. Any tears in a sheet may lengthen and documents may as a result become fragmented. Brittle paper is particularly vulnerable.

A document may come under strain if it is not fully supported and part of it is overhanging the edge of the scanning bed. Imaging will also often require a document to be held against a glass plate or under a lid, which can cause damage if the document is not carefully positioned, and can introduce fresh folds if the document is fastened in the corner. The pressure involved in pushing against a plate or lid can put a strain on bindings and fastenings so that there is a risk of damage, especially if the paper has already been weakened by natural deterioration. Some materials are especially vulnerable to cracking when placed under pressure, such as some photographic materials.

If the process requires the document to travel through a scanner then it may come into contact with rollers or guards, which can leave marks and/or indentations. If a document is passed around a drum in the presence of heat then this might cause deformation and also increases the risk of the document being caught either wholly or partially within the scanner during imaging, possibly causing severe damage. A problem such as a misfeed, machine malfunction or power cut could also result in a document becoming trapped, resulting in damage when removal is attempted.

Exposure to light

The light sources used in imaging systems are more intense than the ambient light used in the office environment. However, light damage is cumulative and depends on the duration of exposure as well as the light level. A study by Blackwell (2002) looked at the light levels in different models of flatbed scanners and found that while some models had light levels of more than 2000 lux the scanning times were so brief that overall exposure was equivalent to less than one hour at 50 lux. Light levels of 50 lux are typically recommended when exhibiting archival materials (Thomson, 1986, 22–3). This is a fraction of the light exposure that a document may receive in a reading room where typical light levels would be around 500 lux. Vitale (1998) assessed lighting during digital photography using light levels of up to 5000 lux for 20 minutes per scan. Even at this level, the degree of exposure is equivalent to only four days at 50 lux.

The risk of light damage during imaging is therefore relatively low but it is still a sensible precaution to minimize light exposure. This can be done by simply avoiding unnecessary exposure; for example, the document should not be left under lights while equipment is being set up and calibrated. To avoid moving the document back and forth it can be kept covered until it is needed. Some lighting systems incorporate a dimmer mechanism that allows light levels to be lowered when full light is not needed. Ultraviolet (UV) light is the most damaging (Thomson, 1986, 15–16) and so light sources should be filtered to exclude it.

Exposure to heat

If an imaging operation is running for long hours, the equipment and lights will become warm or even hot and this will warm up the space around them. Tests carried out at the British Library found that after only a few hours of continuous imaging, the temperature of the glass plate on a flatbed scanner had risen by more than 10°C (Browne, 2001). This would be a risk to materials that are particularly sensitive to heat, such as some photographic materials or parchment. However, the ambient conditions during the same tests were not significantly affected, suggesting that the heating effect is localized. The build up of heat in a workspace will depend on a number of factors such as degree of ventilation, staff numbers and duration of the work-shifts. It is advisable to monitor the environment in the workspace, as much for human comfort as for the welfare of the documents. This is discussed further in Chapter 9 'Setting up the imaging operation'.

Disassociation

This is the risk that documents become mixed up during the imaging process. They can be repacked into the wrong boxes and the sequence of documents can be disturbed so that documents become mislaid, or lose their association with other documents. In a worst case scenario, documents could become lost altogether. This risk should be considered when setting up the workspace and designing the workflow, but it is also a factor when deciding to remove fastenings, which in turn may influence the choice of equipment. If the equipment allows documents to be imaged with fastenings in place then this risk is greatly reduced.

Features to consider
Image specifications

The purpose of the digital images will determine the required image specifications. The image specifications should be determined before equipment is selected (see Chapter 3 'The digital image') so as to ensure that the system will capture images of the required standard. Generally speaking, a high quality image specification will require more expensive equipment.

Speed of image capture

The time taken to capture the digital image is partly determined by the desired resolution, partly by the physical capabilities of the equipment, and partly by the processing abilities of the computer that is supporting the scanner. It is important to find out the time taken to capture an image of the required specification as the scan speed quoted by a manufacturer is likely to be for a low quality A4 image. In general, the higher quality specification for the image, the slower the image-taking process will be.

   When considering the rate of image capture it is also important to take into account the time needed for document handling. Image capture of a collection from a library or archive will almost always involve manual handling of the document, rather than automated handling. Office scanners typically involve automated sheet-feed that can process hundreds of sheets per minute. Even a modest desktop scanner with automated sheet-feed is capable of capturing more than 1000 A4 images in an hour. Some high-end equipment can capture more than 20,000 images per hour. In comparison, when digitizing historic documents where each document is processed by hand, an image capture rate of 1000 images per day is an achievement. For special collections, for example rare manuscripts, a rate of several hundred per week might be more realistic.

The significance of the speed of imaging will depend on the scale of the project. For a large-scale project that involves digitizing many thousands of documents, the rate of image capture will have an impact on the timescale of the whole project and the overall costs. For a project involving fewer than 100 manuscripts it may be less critical. If document handling is going to have a significant impact on the rate of work, then a system that has a very fast capture rate can compensate for this.

Physical limitations

Most scanning equipment is designed to accommodate documents of a maximum size, weight and depth. For some equipment there are also limitations on the weight or density (grams per square metre [gsm]) of the paper. While it may be feasible to compromise on image quality and capture speed in order to economize, there is little flexibility where physical requirements are concerned. For a collection with highly variable material this can present serious difficulties. It is therefore critical that a collection survey is carried out in advance so as to gain a full understanding of the physical attributes of the collection. A collection survey will indicate whether sheets are loose, fastened, bound or rolled, how variable the sizes are, the presence of special items such as seals or photographic materials, and whether the condition of the collection is cause for concern (see Chapter 5 'Surveying collections').

Ideally, scanning equipment should be set up so as to cope with variations in the documents. Experience has shown that even apparently consistent documents will have variations and a survey is not guaranteed to detect all anomalies, especially if only a sample has been assessed. Some variations such as the grain direction of paper will not be immediately apparent but will affect the behaviour of the document when handled. If a scanning operation is set up with no scope to adapt to change then a situation could arise where documents cannot be imaged due to physical limitations.

Specialist equipment is available for some document formats and media such as large format documents and transparent materials. However, some manufacturers are willing to adapt existing equipment so as to accommodate unusual formats. It is therefore worth opening a dialogue with a manufacturer to explore possibilities rather than assuming that specialist equipment is the only option.

Software and ease of use

Image capture equipment will usually come with operating software. This software will be the user interface for adjusting settings and entering metadata. The software will therefore often determine how user-friendly the system is. A sophisticated system will have good functionality but will require a user with a bit more technical experience than a more basic scanner will. Ease of use will affect the staffing of the project and therefore the costs. The skills and knowledge of existing staff should be taken into consideration when choosing equipment.

Operating software can also enable the operator to carry out some post-imaging processing. Types of post processing are described in Chapter 3 'The digital image'. Processing of the digital image is an inevitable part of the digitization process but it does not need to be carried out at the time of image capture. It is therefore not an essential feature of the image capture software. If documents are highly varied then a degree of image processing, such as cropping, can take place at the time of image capture so as to save time later. Alternatively, for documents that require particularly careful handling it may be preferable to focus more on image capture and leave processing for later.

Calibration, as mentioned in Chapter 3 'The digital image', is an important aspect of the set up and maintenance of the imaging equipment. Frey and Reilly (2006, 32–3) provide more detail, suggesting it should be carried out at monthly intervals during the image capture process. There are a variety of methods for calibration and different equipment will have different requirements, requiring different levels of technical expertise. When choosing equipment this should be clarified with the supplier.

Technical support and sustainability

Before purchasing imaging equipment, an institution should consider the need for in-house expertise in order to operate and maintain the equipment. Some scanning systems are very straightforward to set up and use but if a problem should arise in the midst of an imaging operation it could be expensive to have to seek external technical support, not least because of the potential delays this may cause. The purchase of equipment should be part of an overall digitization strategy at an institution so that consideration is given to future use of the equipment and staff development is undertaken in tandem with this.

Cost

When comparing the cost of different imaging systems it is important to also consider the operating costs. It is therefore useful to look at the cost per image, as this will take into account not only the cost of the equipment, but also the scan rate and staff costs for image capture and post-processing. Cost per image is also useful for comparing the cost of outsourcing with the cost of in-house image capture. Hughes (2004, 86–92) provides a useful summary and describes the methodology for calculating cost per image.

The image specification will, to a certain extent, dictate both the choice of equipment and the rate of image capture – both of which will affect the cost per image. However, despite the daunting costs, it would be a false economy to try to save money by capturing at a lower image specification, as the resulting images may be of limited use. It should be remembered that if the project involves text conversion then the cost of imaging the documents makes up a relatively small proportion of the overall project budget. Typically the most expensive element of such a digitization project would be the transcription.

Types of equipment

The scanning industry is now sufficiently mature for there to be a range of products aimed at different sectors of the market. More recently manufacturers have recognized that speed and image quality are not the only criteria that customers may consider and some specialist equipment is now available that has been designed with document safety in mind. This is very much a niche market and so specialized equipment is likely to be more expensive, but by working with a manufacturer it is possible to develop a scanning station to meet the exact requirements of a project. This may pay off through a reduction in preparation time, e.g. bound volumes might be scanned bound rather than having to be disbound before imaging.

Flatbed scanners

In a flatbed scanner, the original is placed face-down onto a glass plate. The imaging device consists of lines of imaging sensors with an integrated light source. During imaging, the device passes beneath the glass plate from one side to the other capturing the image line by line. The scanner has a lid so as to exclude ambient light and so that scanning can be carried out in daylight conditions. Some flatbed scanners can be fitted with an adapter to scan transparent materials via transmitted light.

A flatbed scanner might be suitable for loose sheet material that is robust and in good condition, such as index cards or mounted prints. However, for documents that are A2 sized or larger the capture rate is relatively slow when compared with that of other imaging equipment, and some flatbed scanners require a pre-scan before scanning each image, which will slow down the process even more. Another disadvantage is that with prolonged usage the glass plate will become warm, posing a risk to some heat-sensitive documents, such as some photographic materials.

For many archival and library materials the document handling required for scanning with a flatbed scanner is undesirable. In particular, flatbed scanners are not appropriate for bound volumes or papers that are fastened together. Not only does the lid put pressure on the binding or fastening, but also the document would need to be turned face-down for each image, and then turned face-up again in order to turn to the next page. This extensive handling is both time-consuming and potentially damaging to the item.

Another difficulty is that the operator cannot see the face of the document because it is face down on the glass plate. Any errors are only apparent during pre-scanning or actual image capture, after which the operator must correct the position of the document and then re-scan. This is a problem if the document will not lie flat because a document that wants to curl or fold up is very difficult to control when the operator is trying to close the lid. One way to address this difficulty is to prepare sheets by inserting each one into a polyester sleeve. A simple sleeve, welded along two sides, will support the document during handling and will ensure that the document lies flat during imaging. However, the sleeves would need to be removed after imaging if the documents are not intended to be stored in them. When considering imaging documents inside polyester sleeves, testing should be carried out because there is a risk that light will reflect from the plastic causing glare in the resulting image. The use of polyester sleeves is discussed in full in Chapter 8 'Preparation of damaged documents'.

As with other purpose-built scanning equipment, a flatbed scanner can only accommodate documents of a specific size. If a document is too large then it will not be possible to capture it in one image. An oversized document will hang over the edges of the scanning bed, and may cover the control panel on the scanner. Even if supported, for example by foam blocks, when the lid of the scanner is closed there is still a risk that the edge of the lid will create indentations in the paper and where the lid is hinged the document will not be able to overhang, so this is far from ideal.

Some multifunction scanners are designed without a lid so as to overcome some of the problems with flatbed scanners. The scanner consists of a fixed glass plate with a moveable bed beneath. The imaging device and integrated light source pass across the top of the glass plate. This type of scanner works under ambient light conditions and so has the benefit that the operator can see the document and thus can ensure that it is positioned perfectly before taking the scan. Also, this type of scanner can be used with a book cradle. However, the presence of a fixed glass plate can still be problematic if a document will not lie flat and it is not appropriate for some fastened papers to be under glass, as the glass plate may create fresh folds.

Overhead or planetary scanners

Overhead scanners, also known as planetary scanners, are designed with the imaging device mounted above the scanning bed. Typically, the imaging device consists of lines of sensors as in a flatbed scanner and so the image is captured line by line. However, some systems have been designed with a digital camera and these may also be referred to as planetary scanners. The light source is sometimes integrated into the scanning head so that the light passes across the document as the image is captured, but the light source can also be mounted separately. Sometimes there are two light sources on adjustable arms fixed above the scanning bed on either side. There is a limit to the size of items that an overhead scanner can accommodate. This is because the imaging device is typically in a fixed position with a limited field of vision. The field of vision increases if the imaging device is mounted further away from the scanning bed, therefore an overhead scanner designed to capture sizes larger than A0 will not only have a large scanning bed but may also be large in terms of overall height. The capture speed of overhead scanners can be relatively slow if they capture line by line. The higher the resolution and the larger the document the longer the scan will take. The capture time may be only 10–15 seconds per image, but this still means that it is difficult to capture more than 1000 images per day.

In terms of document handling, overhead scanners are often promoted as being ideal for the digitization of fragile and historic documents, the main advantages being that the document lies face-up on the scanning bed and contact with the scanner is minimal. In addition, many overhead scanners come with a book cradle that will not only fully support a bound volume but will also compensate for the shift in the volume's profile as it is digitized. Some overhead scanners can be fitted with a glass plate so that documents can be held flat during image capture if necessary. If the plate is hinged then it can be lifted out of the way when not needed. When a bound volume is digitized without a glass plate, the curvature at the spine edge of the page can result in a shadow or distortion of the lines of text. This can be corrected digitally after image capture and some scanners come with software to do this. More recently, specialized book scanners have been designed to address this issue (see the section 'Specialized scanners' below).

Digital cameras

One of the main advantages of a digital camera is that the imaging sensors are arranged in a matrix rather than in a line and so the digital image can be captured instantly. Another significant advantage is that the scanning station consists of a light source and the camera on a copy stand or tripod, and so is both simple and flexible. The camera can be raised or lowered to change the field of view and thus accommodate documents of different sizes. Likewise the light sources can be moved so as to achieve the best results. As with an overhead scanner, using a digital camera requires minimal contact with the document. A copy stand can be used with or without a book cradle and so a variety of document formats can be successfully imaged, from objects such as seals to large format sheet material such as maps.

A digital camera is not necessarily the cheapest choice of equipment because in order to capture images of sufficient quality a camera with a digital back or scanback is needed. A compact digital camera would not provide images of suitable format or quality. Setting up, adjusting and maintaining the equipment may also require more technical expertise when compared with scanners, which can be operated with minimal introductory training. Ideally, the imaging should be carried out by someone with photographic experience. However, when considering the costs per image a digital camera is an attractive option due to speed of image capture, and from a preservation perspective it offers a safe way to image a range of document formats and materials.

Sheet-feed scanners

A sheet-feed scanner is designed with a fixed imaging device and light source. The document is pulled through the machine by rollers so that it passes over the imaging device. The paper path can be straight, so that the sheet remains horizontal as it passes through the machine, or it can be curved. As previously mentioned there is a risk of physical damage when a document is passed through a scanning machine. However there are advantages to automated sheet-feed when digitization on a large scale is being undertaken. Some sheet-feed scanners are capable of duplex scanning where both sides of the sheet are captured at the same time. This, in combination with the automated process, means that a high volume of documents can be scanned very quickly. The system can work well for projects where the sheets are very consistent in size and weight so long as the documents are checked and prepared before scanning to remove all attachments such as paperclips and insert any damaged sheets into polyester sleeves. See Chapter 8 'Preparation of damaged documents' for more on the use of polyester sleeves during image capture.

CASE STUDY: 1911 census records

The 1911 census records consisted of more than 35,000 bound volumes of census schedules – the forms returned by each individual household during the 1911 census of England and Wales. The collection was extremely large, but also highly consistent and so sheet-feed scanners were chosen for the image capture. The chosen scanner was capable of capturing 320 images per minute (A4 duplex scans) but for the digitization project it was operated at its slowest speed of 1000 images per hour (Ahmon, 2008, 27) to capture 24-bit colour images approximately A3 in size at 200 DPI. The scanner was set with a horizontal paper path so that the documents did not pass around a drum. Another feature of the scanner was that it was designed so that it could be opened up to easily gain access to the paper path. Each scanner

was equipped with an uninterruptible power supply (UPS) so that, in the event of a power failure, it would complete its current scan. Every document was checked and prepared as necessary before being scanned. See Chapter 7 'Preparation of document formats and fastenings' and Chapter 8 'Preparation of damaged documents' for more on the preparation of documents during this project.

The National Archives UK catalogue reference: RG 14 General Register Office:
    1911 Census Schedules
Online at www.1911census.co.uk

Drum scanners

Drum scanners use a different type of image sensor than other types of document scanners and can capture digital images of exceptionally high resolution and quality (DPI of several thousands). Image capture at such a high resolution is relatively slow. The original document must be attached to a drum inside the machine, which is then rotated at high speed past the imaging device. Drum scanners are expensive and are typically found in professional scanning bureaux where they are mainly used for the design and reprographic industries. In particular they are often used to scan photographic transparencies where particularly high resolution is needed so that images can be enlarged and reproduced to a high standard. Due to the specialized nature of drum scanners they are generally not suitable for library and archive materials. In particular the practice of wet mounting photographic transparent materials onto the drum would be problematic for archival material.

Specialized scanners
'V'-shaped book scanners

A handful of manufacturers have sought to address the need for high volume book scanning by designing highly specialized equipment. A common feature of such book scanning systems is a 'V'-shaped book cradle. This has the advantage that the book is open at an angle and does not need to be completely flat during the image capture. This puts less of a strain on the binding structure and so is better for the welfare of the document but it also means that image capture is slightly faster because page turning is fractionally quicker. Images are captured by a pair of digital cameras angled towards the recto and verso pages. Alternatively, the imaging device is integrated into a 'V'-shaped scanning head that is inserted into the open angle of the book. Both of these approaches to imaging address the problem of shadows and curvature in the spine edge of the book, which can affect the legibility of the digital image.

Robotic book scanners

Robotic book scanners introduce automated page turning to speed up the process. Different manufacturers have come up with different solutions for page turning, such as employing blown air, robotic arms and a complex array of sensors to detect the page edge and folds. Robotic book scanners often incorporate a 'V'-shaped book cradle. Manufacturers claim that robotic book scanners can scan thousands of pages an hour, compared with the hundreds per hour that can be achieved when scanning by hand. This option could be considered for library digitization so long as the condition of books was assessed before digitization. However, archival materials may pose problems; for example an automated system would not be able to scan items that were folded inside a volume or pasted into a volume.

Large format scanners

Large format scanners are sheet-feed scanners designed specifically for the digitization of large-scale maps, plans and drawings of size A0 and larger. They are usually designed to be freestanding so that the document is fed into the machine by hand and passes out the other end. The advantage of this design is that it is relatively compact and takes up much less room than a scanner with a flat bed. However, as with all automatic feed systems there is a risk of physical damage when the document passes through the scanner. With large format scanners there is an additional risk because if the document is not supported when it emerges from the back of the scanner it will hang down vertically and may end up trailing on the floor. Nevertheless, such scanners can be the best solution for a collection of large-scale items that are in consistently good condition.

Scanning transparent media

Some flatbed scanners are designed with an additional light source integrated into the lid so that it is possible to scan using transmitted light. Scanner accessories are also available that will hold several slides or negative strips so that it is possible to digitize several items in one pass. For the mass digitization of a consistent format it may be economical to use a specialist transparency scanner. These are designed to capture a small area at high resolution but might not be suitable for fragile materials as scanning may need to involve sliding the original item into the device resulting in scratches or other physical damage.

Selecting and testing

There is unlikely to be one imaging system that can meet all the digitization needs of an institution with a highly varied collection. It may therefore be necessary to establish a suite of imaging systems, for example, the Munich Digitization Center now has more than half a dozen different types of scanning systems, including robotic book scanners, digital cameras and a scanner specifically designed to scan watermarks (Munich Digitization Center, 2010). Outsourcing is another way to achieve a versatile imaging operation. A supplier will already have the relevant equipment and may be able to provide different systems as necessary, for example, the contractor for the Library of Congress' National Digital Library Program made use of digital cameras, flatbed scanners and book scanners (Library of Congress, 1999). Chapter 2 'Before you digitize: resources, suppliers and surrogates' discusses some of the pros and cons of outsourcing.

If an institution with no previous experience of digital imaging is considering investing in imaging equipment they would be wise to seek independent advice so as to avoid making a costly mistake. Broadly speaking, when choosing equipment you get what you pay for. High-end, sophisticated equipment is likely to be the most expensive. However, the technical specifications provided by different manufacturers often defy direct comparison; for example, digital cameras describe resolution differently from scanning systems. Williams (2000, Section 4.4) offers some guidance on how to interpret equipment specifications. Again, outsourcing can be the solution for an institution that lacks the technical expertise. It will also simplify matters by removing the need to deal with problems that require technical support (unless there are issues with the institution's IT systems) and through removing concerns over the long-term sustainability of the operation. Chapter 2 'Before you digitize: resources, suppliers and surrogates' discusses some of the factors to bear in mind when working with suppliers.

However, whether an institution is building an in-house facility or has decided to outsource, the minimum requirements must be defined. Gertz (2000) provides a list of specifications that should be drafted when approaching potential suppliers, and many of the same specifications are needed when shopping for equipment. The key elements are the image specifications and the physical requirements. It is therefore essential that the project is thoroughly scoped before equipment is selected or suppliers are approached. This includes carrying out a collection survey (see Chapter 5 'Surveying collections') so that physical requirements are fully described. For example, if a collection includes a proportion of items that are over A1 in size then this should be quantified.

Testing is the best way to demonstrate that the specifications have been understood and are satisfied. The approach to testing should be in proportion to the project, so it may involve a visit and an equipment demonstration, or at the other extreme may require a more extensive pilot project. A combination of dummy documents and original documents can be used, depending on what is being tested. For example, a dummy document may be sufficient to demonstrate the delivery of the required image specification, whereas original documents would be needed to test handling issues.

Finally, manufacturers and suppliers will often publicize their client list, so if this list includes a comparable institution it may be worthwhile making contact with them. In general it is worth speaking to colleagues in other institutions who are implementing digitization. They are sure to be willing to share their experiences, good and bad.

Chapter summary

- The image specification must be defined and the physical attributes of the documents must be investigated via a collection survey before choosing the equipment for image capture.
- The physical attributes of the documents will influence the choice of

equipment, but this is only one of several features that need to be considered.

- Fast image capture can compensate for the time involved in careful handling of the documents.
- During image capture, the greatest risk to the original documents is physical damage through handling.
- Overhead imaging systems offer flexibility and are generally good for document welfare as the imaging device does not need to be in direct contact with the document.

Bibliography

Ahmon, J. (2008) Digitisation of 1911 Census Schedules, *ICON News: the magazine of the Institute of Conservation*, **14** (January), 25–8.

Blackwell, B. (2002) Light Exposure to Sensitive Artworks during Digital Photography, *WAAC (Western Association for Art Conservation) Newsletter*, **22** (3), http://cool.conservation-us.org/waac/wn/wn24/wn24-3/wn24-306.html.

Browne, M. (2001) *Scanning Equipment: the reliability of thermometer strips with an additional report on the heat generated and radiated by a working standard office scanner*, SEPIA (Safeguarding European Photographic Images for Access) Work Package 4/3, www.knaw.nl/ecpa/sepia/workinggroups/wp4/ScanningEquipment.pdf.

Frey, F. S. and Reilly, J. M. (2006) *Digital Imaging for Photographic Collections: foundations for technical standards: second edition*, Image Permanence Institute, www.imagepermanenceinstitute.org/shtml_sub/digibook.pdf.

Gertz, J. (2000) Vendor Relations. In Sitts, M. K. (ed.), *Handbook for Digital Projects: a management tool for preservation and access: first edition*, Northeast Document Conservation Centre, www.nedcc.org/resources/digitalhandbook/viii.htm.

Hughes, L. (2004) *Digitizing Collections: strategic issues for the information manager*, Facet Publishing.

Library of Congress (1999) *Conservation Implications of Digitization Projects*, National Digital Library Program and the Conservation Division, http://lcweb2.loc.gov/ammem/techdocs/conserv83199a.pdf.

Munich Digitization Center (2010) *The Scanning Equipment of the Munich Digitization Center*, www.digital-collections.de/index.html?c=digitalisierung-scanner&l=en.

Thomson, G. (1986) *The Museum Environment,* 2nd edn, Butterworth-Heinemann.

Vitale, T. (1998) Light Levels Used in Modern Flatbed Scanners, *RLG (Research Libraries Group) DigiNews,* **2** (5), http://worldcat.org/arcviewer/1/OCC/2007/08/08/0000070511/viewer/file3642.html#technical.

Williams, D. (2000) Selecting a Scanner. In Colet, L. S., D'Amato, D., Frey, F. and Williams, D. (eds), *Guides to Quality in Visual Resource Imaging,* DLF (Digital Library Federation), CLIR (Council on Library and Information Resources), RLG (Research Libraries Group), www.diglib.org/pubs/dlf091.

7

Preparation of document formats and fastenings

Introduction

As discussed in Chapter 6 'Equipment for image capture' the physical attributes of a collection will influence the choice of equipment. However, even if the most suitable equipment has been selected many collections will still need to be prepared in some way before digitization. Preparation consists of dealing with any aspects of the document format and condition that will interfere with the image capture. It ensures that items are ready for imaging, can be safely handled and that good quality images are captured. Preparing documents for image capture will add to the timescale and budget of a project but with careful planning and good management it can be incorporated smoothly into the workflow of an operation and will help the project run more efficiently. If preparation is nonexistent, inadequate or poorly planned, this can result in repeated delays at the imaging stage and/or in a poor quality, incomplete digital surrogate.

This chapter looks at preparing different document formats and fastened documents while Chapter 8 'Preparation of damaged documents' focuses on conservation work to deal with damaged documents. Although formats, fastenings and damaged documents are considered separately, the two chapters should be considered together because there are similar themes running through both, in particular the issue of how to fit document preparation into the workflow. All examples used in these two chapters are based on projects carried out at The National Archives UK.

Preparing formats and fastenings

Formats and fastenings often cause difficulties during image capture because they can make documents awkward to handle and may restrict a document so that it will not open easily. The rate of capture can be drastically reduced if an operator is having to deal with complex housings or fastenings, or having to unfold or unroll individual items in order to take an image. With mixed collections of documents a combination of different issues may be encountered. The initial spot check assessment of a collection, as described in Chapter 4 'The process of selection', should indicate if there are potential problems with the documents and also how variable the collection is. The collection survey will then quantify these issues. See Chapter 5 'Surveying collections' for more on collection surveys and what to look for. Once the scope of the problems is understood, decisions can be made regarding what preparation is needed, who will do this work and how this will fit into the imaging operation.

Preparation of formats and fastenings should be considered carefully because it can involve permanent changes. It might not be possible to reassemble some types of fastenings or housings once they have been dismantled, for example if bindings must be cut in order to be taken apart. This could result in original material being permanently removed or altered in some way. For a collection where preservation of the documents is of paramount importance, original material should be preserved as far as possible. The collection manager should therefore take a pragmatic approach, balancing the needs of the digitization project with the long-term impact on the documents. Preparation can be done in such a way as to benefit documents if it results in improvements in housing or the removal of rusty metal fastenings.

There are many other inter-related factors to take into consideration as well as issues of long-term preservation. These factors are examined in more detail below for dealing with fastenings, bundles of folded papers and rolls, and bindings.

Fastenings

A brief history of stationery would reveal a huge variety of methods and materials used to fasten documents together, many of which are encountered in collections of historic documents. This includes paperclips, pins, staples and treasury tags (see Figure 7.1) as well as strings and ribbons. Items were not only attached by way of a fastening but were also sometimes glued together or attached using whatever resources were to hand at the time, such as self-

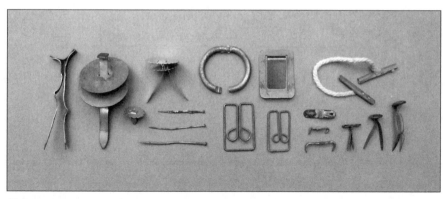

Figure 7.1 *An assortment of different fastenings*

adhesive postage stamps, labels or seals. Fastenings can cause damage to documents as they age: adhesive tape that has aged may cause permanent stains; rusting metal fastenings can cause permanent discolouration and weaken the paper structurally through oxidization processes. For the purposes of digitization, fastenings can be problematic for a number of reasons.

- Documents which are clipped or pinned together will not lie flat.
- Documents can be fastened in such as way as to obscure information (see Figure 7.2).
- A damaged document fastened to other documents must be handled with particular care (see Figure 7.3 on the next page).
- Metal fastenings can scratch parts of the image-capturing equipment, such as glass plates.

However, if fastenings are present and pose these problems it should not be automatically assumed that they need to be removed. There may be situations where, all things considered, the costs and risks outweigh the benefits of removing fastenings. It is possible to achieve good results with fastened

Figure 7.2 *The stapled corner obscures text*

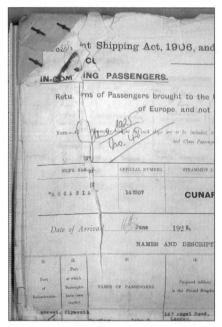

documents by using appropriate equipment and handling methods.

Impact of removal on preservation and context

Fastenings are used for good reason: to keep associated documents together and to keep items in sequence. When fastenings are removed there is therefore a risk that the loose papers may get out of sequence, lose their original arrangement and context and lose some of their meaning as a result; for example, a memo pinned to correspondence may have limited meaning once it is detached. Smaller items are particularly vulnerable and there is a greater risk of loss once fastenings are removed. It may be

Figure 7.3 *The damaged sheet is more difficult to handle because it is fastened to other sheets*

appropriate to consult with an archivist on the risk of disassociation and the impact that this would have on the collection.

Fastened documents can be easier to handle than loose sheets, especially if sheets are of different sizes. This can mean that the handling during image capture is quicker and easier with fastenings in place, but it is also important to consider future users who will consult the collection. The removal of fastenings can also have implications for the long-term preservation of items if it means that covers are detached and so documents are no longer well protected. These issues may not seem to be particularly relevant in the immediate future when the digital surrogate will be used in place of the original documents, but when considering the preservation and future access of the collection a long-term view should be adopted. This means considering the next 50 to 100 years of the collection, rather than the next five or ten.

A fastening might be an original part of a document and in general removal of any original material should be avoided because this will adversely affect the authenticity of an item. However, a fastening is not always original and may be a later addition. If there is doubt about whether or not a fastening is original then the item should be assessed by a conservator. There may be instances where it is appropriate to remove original fastenings, for example, if metal fastenings are rusty or if fastenings would put a strain on damaged documents. Such decisions should be made by a conservator, who should also consider if the original fastenings should be preserved because they are rare or significant. If fastenings are considered to be significant in themselves – for instance, if they are of great antiquity – then it may be possible for a conservator to remove them and then replace them after imaging. However, this may be a time-consuming operation, in which case it should only be done after all other options have been considered and rejected.

Options for dealing with obscured text

Given that the preservation and context of items would be at risk once fastenings are removed, it is worth considering alternative options. If text is obscured by the fastening, the number and significance of the words affected should be considered; the loss of a few words may not diminish the overall meaning of the document, and if only parts of words are missing then it may still be possible to understand their meaning within the context. Also taken into consideration should be whether the same information is repeated elsewhere; for example, if this is one of a set of standard forms.

The overall impact on the user will depend on the context of use. For example, even if significant words are illegible this may not be such a problem if a transcription is also available. If the end-user will view the document in the context of other associated material the loss of text is likely to have less impact than if an end-user is paying to download a single image. For example, the document seen in Figure 7.2 is a list of passengers who were on board a ship. The most significant word that is lost is the name of the ship, 'Melita', which is partially obscured at the top of the sheet. However, the user could obtain this name from a transcription of the list or from an image of the front page of the list where the ship's name would be clearly visible.

There may be further ways to compensate for missing text via the online presentation. The online service can include contextual information to assist the user in the interpretation of documents. If documents are standard forms then one way of compensating for missing words is to display a sample blank form so that users can see the content that may be missing from individual images. It is also a good idea to manage the user's expectations by making it clear that the document format has affected the image quality in some cases. This is particularly important for a pay-per-view payment model.

Imaging with fastenings in place

Fastened documents can be successfully imaged with the fastenings in place if suitable equipment is used. See Chapter 6 'Equipment for image capture' for an overview of different types of equipment. A sheet-feed scanner cannot be used and flatbed scanners and scanners with a glass plate may also pose difficulties because the processes should not introduce fresh creases into the document. An overhead system such as a planetary scanner or a digital camera on a stand offers the most flexible set-up. It may be the case that equipment is already in place and cannot be changed but it may still be possible to successfully image the documents without removing the fastenings. It may be feasible to untie and loosen fastenings to facilitate imaging without needing to remove the fastenings altogether. This may be possible for documents tied with ribbons or strings, although if a fastening is loosened then the item can be difficult to handle.

Weights can be used to hold down an item that will not lie flat (see Figure 7.4), leaving both hands free to operate the equipment. Specialist weights are commercially available, known as book weights. They are in the form of a small bag/pouch made of cloth/leather and containing lead shot or a string of lead beads in a cloth casing. The latter are sometimes called snake weights. Weighting tape for curtains would do the same job, as would small glass weights (see Figure 7.5). Weights should be clean and should not mark the document, so a weight with a painted coating would be unsuitable.

This approach may not be feasible if the item is too large or too heavy. Another disadvantage is that it may be unavoidable for the weights to appear in the resulting image. A series of test images could be taken to see how the weights work in practice and whether the resulting images are acceptable to all parties.

When imaging with fastenings in place it may be necessary to mask off documents that are visible in the background. This can be done simply by inserting a blank sheet (either white or black) behind the document being

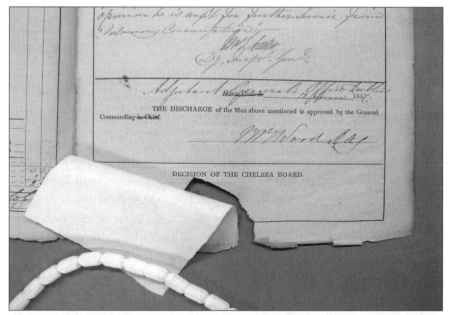

Figure 7.4 *Use of a snake weight to hold down a document*

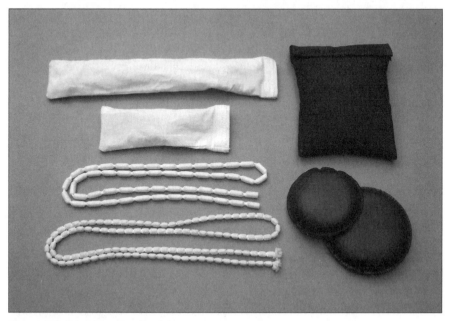

Figure 7.5 *Suitable types of weights*

imaged so that the documents behind are covered up. The alternative approach is to crop the image afterwards. Cropping is a type of post processing (see Chapter 3 'The digital image'). This would add a step to the image processing but means that the image capture is slightly faster.

Removal, refastening and rehousing

It is important to consider how easy it is to remove the fastenings because this will determine whether or not the work needs to be done by a conservator or if the imaging operator can do it, and how long the work will take. This in turn will affect the resources required and how the work will fit into the imaging operation, issues which are discussed later. For example, paperclips are likely to pose few problems as they can be slipped off at the time of imaging while for some other metal fastenings (such as staples) hand tools are needed. Some fastenings may prove difficult to remove without causing damage to the document in which case the item should be assessed by a conservator. Ease of removal may therefore have a bearing when deciding whether or not to remove fastenings at all. If fastenings can only be removed using hand tools or if removal poses a significant risk of damage to the document then it may be preferable to leave them in place.

Equally important is whether or not the items will be refastened and if so, whether the original fastenings can be re-used. If fastenings have been removed then it is preferable to refasten documents after imaging because this will address many of the risks previously mentioned such as disassociation and loss. Paperclips are easy to re-use and if the documents are refastened immediately after imaging the risks are minimized. Similarly, it may be possible to re-use strings and ribbons. However, some fastenings cannot be re-used, for example strings which have been cut, or staples; also there may be reasons why it is preferable not to re-use some fastenings, for example if they are rusty or too tight. It may therefore be necessary to refasten items in some other way.

When refastening documents the method should ideally not introduce fresh holes so stapling items together or punching holes in items should be avoided. In some instances it may be possible to re-use existing holes, for example if an old treasury tag is cut and removed then a fresh one can be inserted after imaging using the same holes. Paperclips offer an ideal fastening in most cases, although they may not be feasible for very thick documents, or may be undesirable if it means that the collection will contain thousands of paperclips (some of which may fall off). An alternative would be to use folders or paper wrappers to keep associated papers together. If necessary individual sheets can be enumerated so that the sequence can be maintained. The options for dealing with different fastenings are summarized in Table 7.1.

Table 7.1 *Summary of options for removal of fastenings*

Fastening	Method	By whom
Paperclip	Remove by hand at time of imaging and replace after imaging.	Operator
Staple	Remove using hand tool and replace with paperclip or house papers in folder.	Conservator or operator under supervision
Pin	Remove by hand at time of imaging and replace with paperclip or house papers in folder.	Operator
Treasury tag	Remove by hand at time of imaging and replace after imaging. Alternatively cut off at time of imaging and replace with fresh tag after imaging.	Operator
Strings/ribbon	If possible untie and loosen then leave in place during imaging. Tighten and retie after imaging. If string/ribbon needs to be removed then untie, retain original string/ribbon and retie after imaging, or, cut off at time of imaging and replace with paperclip or house papers in folder.	Conservator may be needed to undo and tie original string/ribbon. If fastening is cut this can be done by operator
Glued items	If possible, and if appropriate, remove using moisture or solvents. Replace with paperclip or house papers in folder.	Conservator

Resources required and impact on workflow

The task of removing fastenings from documents can be a daunting undertaking because a mass digitization project can involve processing tens of thousands of documents. A collection of 2000 boxes consisting of 50 stapled documents per box would contain 100,000 staples – and this assumes only one staple per document. The removal of fastenings is work that must be done by hand and with care not to tear the documents. For a large-scale project it may necessitate additional staff to prepare the documents and this would need to be incorporated into the plans for the imaging operation as it will have an impact on the workflow.

These considerations will also apply to smaller projects involving hundreds rather than thousands of documents because dealing with fastenings will still add time to the process and may need to involve the services of a conservator. The resources required to deal with the fastenings may therefore be disproportionate to the scale of the project. For these reasons it may be worth considering whether or not removal is absolutely necessary, for instance if fastenings can be left in place by choosing different equipment for image capture then this may be preferable. A pilot project or tests would indicate the time and resources needed and would inform the decision to remove fastenings or leave them in place.

Fastenings that are easily removed from documents that are in good condition can be removed by the operator at the time of imaging. Operators can also remove more difficult fastenings, such as rusty items, if they have received training. Any work involving hand tools should ideally be carried out by a conservator, but it can be done by a trained operator who is under the supervision of a conservator. See Table 7.1 for a summary of the options.

More delicate tasks should always be carried out by a conservator, such as removal and subsequent restringing of original ties. If documents have been glued together then separation should be carried out by a conservator because of the need to use moisture and solvents to release the adhesive. It may be too time-consuming to separate them, and the separation may cause damage to the documents. There may also be occasions where an insert has been stuck down deliberately as a correction. The decision to separate such items must therefore be taken by a conservator, taking into account the original intention.

If fastenings are removed then this may involve not only a preparation stage in the imaging operation, but also a post-processing stage when the loose documents are refastened or rehoused. Again, this should be clarified when the project is in development so that it can be incorporated into the planned workflow. Rehousing will require the purchase of materials and may also involve labelling of new housings, writing document reference numbers on folders and securing ties around wrappers. These activities can be time-consuming and so should be accounted for at the planning stage. They also should be done in a manner that is in keeping with the institution's policies on cataloguing and storage.

CASE STUDY: Arrivals passenger lists

The arrivals passenger lists recorded passengers arriving on ships at major UK ports from 1878 to 1960. The lists varied in size and type of paper due to variations over time and differences between different shipping companies since each company was responsible for submitting a list for each ship. The length of the list also varied considerably according to how many passengers were listed, so for a large cruise liner the list could consist of dozens of sheets.

At the planning stage a survey was carried out on a sample of the collection and this indicated that there was a vast array of different fastenings. This included tags, strings, ribbon, paperclips, pins and staples in many different arrangements – in the corner, along the top or down the side. The majority of fastenings did not impede the imaging of the document or obscure any text but metal fastenings were sometimes rusty and causing stains. It was proposed to image the collection using digital cameras on copy stands.

The fastenings were distributed widely throughout the collection and so it was felt that their removal would add a significant amount of work to the project without bringing significant benefit. In fact in some cases the sheets would be easier to handle if they remained fastened. A fastening was only removed if it restricted the opening of a document or if text was obscured. The decision to remove a fastening was initially taken by the project conservator who was working alongside the camera team and removal was carried out by the conservator if necessary. Sometimes it was possible to loosen the fastening rather than remove it altogether. If a fastening was removed then a paperclip was used to keep the sheets together.

This approach was possible because a project conservator was working in the same area as the imaging team and so was available to deal with fastenings on an *ad hoc* basis. As the project progressed and the camera team gained experience of the documents and different fastenings they were able to decide whether or not to remove fastenings and carry out removal themselves. The project conservator was on hand to advise at all times.

The National Archives UK catalogue reference: BT 26 Board of Trade: Commercial and Statistical Departments and Successors: Inward Passenger Lists

Online at http://search.ancestry.co.uk/search/db.aspx?dbid=1518

Bundles of folded papers and rolls

A collection consisting of folded or rolled items does not necessarily require special preparation or equipment in order to capture good images. Any item that will not lie flat can be imaged under a glass plate so as to flatten folds or curvature that may cause shadows and/or distortion of the text. However, as already mentioned, the handling of such formats can be extremely challenging and can have a significant impact on the image capture rate. Documents that have been folded for most of their life may be extremely resistant to being opened and flattened. There is also a risk of causing damage, particularly if the paper is weak along the creases. In addition, time will be needed to unpack items and then repack them after imaging. Some housings can be intricate, such as correspondence that is folded several times and kept in original envelopes. When dealing with rolled items, packing the item after imaging may take longer than unpacking if the item must be rolled so as to fit into a particular housing.

Preparation of folded items

If there is a large quantity of folded items it may be efficient to prepare them by unpacking and unfolding them in advance of imaging. The main advantage of this is that the documents have a chance to relax and so are more likely to stay flat when handled. This applies to both paper and parchment, and will also apply to rolled items. If the collection survey suggests that some items are damaged then unpacking and unfolding presents an opportunity for a conservator to assess items for damage and treat them as necessary. It is possible to adopt a combined approach where a conservator carries out treatments while supervising a team of technicians or assistants to carry out the more routine tasks of unpacking.

When considering the timescales involved, it is worth carrying out a pilot study to provide estimates of time and resources. The size, format and condition of items will dictate requirements such as the materials needed for preparation, such as heavy weights, and whether the preparation should take place in a conservation studio or in proximity to the imaging operation. For example, large format sheet materials such as rolled maps should be prepared near to the imaging area so as to avoid having to transport them around the building.

Factors to consider when rehousing

If unpacking and unfolding in advance of imaging, it is worth considering permanently rehousing the collection rather than repacking the collection as before. The decision to permanently rehouse needs careful consideration because it involves losing the original format, and therefore possibly losing original associations and also original materials. However, rehousing can improve long-term access and preservation if the existing housing is restrictive.

A digitization project can be an excellent opportunity to rehouse a collection because it will involve handling each individual item at least once. Rehousing will also mean that prepared items will be protected during storage and transit for the period between preparation and imaging. This is important because unpacking and unfolding is best carried out with a generous lead-in time so that documents have the maximum amount of time to relax. With this in mind, one option is for rehousing to be carried out at the time of the collection survey. Any conservation work that is identified at the time can be carried out at a later date as part of the imaging operation. This has the advantage of reducing handling since rehousing and condition assessment happen at the same time.

CASE STUDY: Dutch Sailing Letters pilot project

The collection of Dutch Sailing Letters includes boxes of papers from intercepted foreign ships from 1652 to 1811. Six boxes of 18th-century papers were digitized as a pilot project. The boxes were chosen, in part, due to their varied condition and format (see Figure 7.6 for an example) and from the outset it was difficult to estimate how much work would be needed to prepare the papers for imaging. It was eventually decided that all papers should be unfolded, cleaned, repaired as necessary and rehoused prior to imaging. The rehoused papers are no longer in their original format (see Figure 7.7) and this has resulted in the apparent loss of original associations, but in some instances these associations were already unclear because papers had become detached or shuffled within the box.

During the rehousing, great care was taken to maintain known associations, as far as possible using paper wrappers to keep papers and envelopes together and with polyester enclosures being used to house original strings and ribbons. The prepared papers were much easier to

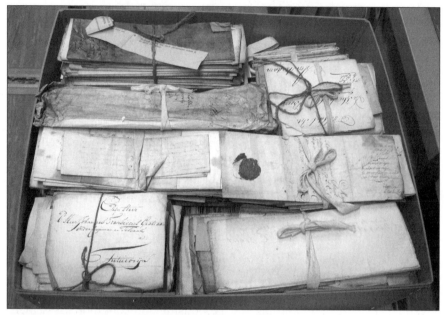

Figure 7.6 *Dutch Sailing Letters before preparation*

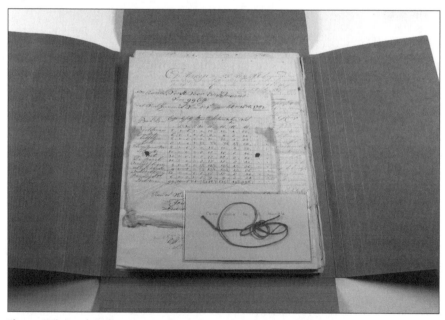

Figure 7.7 *Dutch Sailing Letters after being prepared for digitization*

handle during imaging and in their current format are more readily accessible to future researchers. The preparation work was carried out by a project conservator and took approximately 10% longer than the original estimate, so the pilot project has proved to be invaluable experience that will inform future projects.

The National Archives UK catalogue reference: HCA 30 High Court of Admiralty, and Supreme Court of Judicature, High Court of Justice, Probate, Divorce and Admiralty Division: Admiralty Miscellanea

Online at www.kb.nl/sl

Bindings

Printed books can be the most trouble-free of document formats to digitize. However, within an archival context, books come in many forms and there is a distinction between stationery items that received entries (such as journals, registers and indexes), and volumes that consist of loose papers that have been bound together. The former are purpose-made books made from folds of paper of the same grade and quality and cut to size. The latter are more likely to be associated documents, such as correspondence, and may vary widely in size and in the weight, quality and condition of the paper (see Figure 5.8). Binding styles can include papers tied between covers, various designs of post binding and many variations of sewing styles.

The advantage of housing papers in bound format rather than as loose sheets is that a binding keeps them in sequence and secure. A bound volume is also much easier to handle and consult than loose sheets. Experience at The National Archives UK has shown that loose papers suffer more damage from handling than bound papers, usually in the form of edge damage. However, as discussed previously, one common problem with bindings is that the item will not lie flat when open because of the binding style. This can mean that text near to the spine edge is difficult to read because of the distortion of the page due to curvature, or because of a shadow cast by curvature of the page. In some cases text is missing because it is lost in the binding. This occurs when text extends to the very edge of the sheet. When the loose sheets are sewn together this text becomes hidden underneath the sewing (see Figure 7.8). This can be a problem with the technique known as oversewing (also known as library

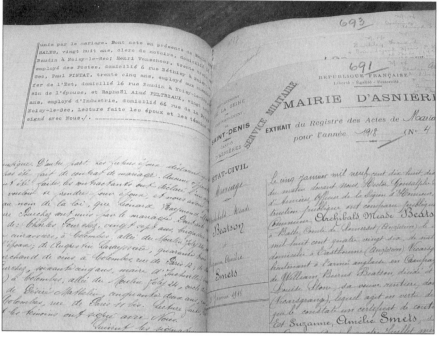

Figure 7.8 *Text is lost where it is hidden underneath sewing*

sewing). But it is a problem with any kind of side sewing, and many types of metal binder.

As with fastenings, if obscured text is the main problem then it is worth considering other options for dealing with it, such as providing an online transcription. If disbinding is proposed there are many factors to consider and the benefits should be weighed carefully against the costs and risks. The removal of bindings will have an impact not only on resources and timescales, but also on the long-term preservation and use of the collection.

Impact of disbinding on preservation and context

Disbinding can be a very destructive process and in most cases a binding cannot be replaced in the way that a simple fastening can. The general approach taken in the office environment would be to remove the cover of a book and guillotine the spine so that the item can be scanned as loose sheets through a sheet-feed scanner. This is not only highly efficient but will also avoid problems at the spine edge of the book. However, this involves the removal of original material and once this material has been removed it cannot easily be re-used. Even if disbinding were to be carried out in a less destructive way, retaining original material as far as possible, for many historic collections this would still not be acceptable simply because the bindings are an integral part of the documents and may themselves be of historical significance. Indeed it may be the institution's policy not to disbind. If a binding is not original material, for example if it is a more recent housing, then disbinding might be acceptable. However, it is not always easy to identify original bindings and so the collection manager should be consulted at the outset.

When disbinding a book that is constructed from sewn folds of paper (such as a stationery binding) there is a significant risk of loss of sequence. This is because each section of a book is made up of several folds of paper. When the section is dismantled it is apparent that most of the individual folded sheets consist of pages that are not in numerical order. Figure 7.9 shows a schematic section constructed from four folds. If these folds were imaged flat then page 1 would appear next to page 16 and page 2 would be next to page 15.

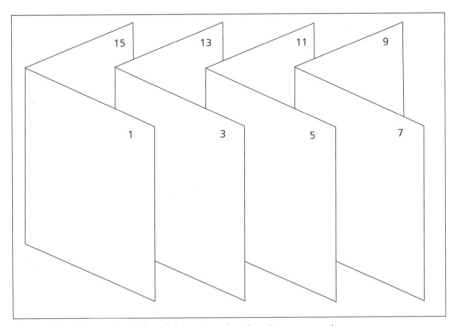

Figure 7.9 *Schematic of a four-fold section showing the page numbers*

In order to maintain the correct sequence the images would need to be cropped and then re-sorted after imaging. This could be avoided by cutting the folds into separate pages but the loose pages would then need to be sorted into numerical order. This option is also far from ideal because it involves the destruction of original material. A less destructive option would be to disbind but maintain the arrangement of folds and sections so that the pages appear in the correct sequence during imaging. This is particularly important if pages are not numbered and so the sequence is not easily apparent.

Imaging restrictive bindings

If bindings are removed then the choice of image capture equipment is wider. However, items can still be imaged successfully with restrictive bindings in place by adapting the scanning station or by using specialist equipment and software. When imaging bound volumes, the imaging equipment should include a book cradle so that the binding is fully supported during imaging. For items that do not lie flat when open, a scanner with a glass plate in combination with a book cradle may be sufficient to get the best images. It may be necessary to test the item on the equipment to ensure that the binding is not under strain as too much pressure could cause the sewing to break. Lighting can be adjusted to minimize shadows at the spine and if curvature is a problem then this can be corrected digitally after image capture. Some image capture software will be able to do this and some book scanners have this function built in.

It may be possible to adapt the workstation so that the book can be imaged when open at an angle. With the volume supported in a book cradle, a digital camera can be angled at either recto or verso. If it is necessary to capture both recto and verso then two cameras can be used, or the volume can be imaged twice – once for recto then again for verso, turning the book around for the second time. Some specialist book scanners are designed in this configuration with a 'V'-shaped book cradle and glass plate, and with lighting and imaging devices positioned at an angle (see Chapter 6 'Equipment for image capture'). For a large collection of bindings it would be worth considering such specialist equipment, although there will be a limit as to the size of items that can be accommodated. Also, being highly specialized, such scanners are unlikely to work with other formats and so when imaging a mixed collection a more flexible solution would be preferable.

Removal, rebinding and rehousing

There are numerous styles of binding, some of which will be simple to remove and replace. More detailed descriptions of binding styles can be found in Roberts and Etherington (1982). If items are to be disbound then they should be rebound or rehoused after imaging so as to maintain the security of the sheets and to maintain their sequence. Loose sheets can be housed in paper wrappers or folders and enumerated so that the sequence is maintained. However, it should also be considered that disbinding volumes will generate a great quantity of loose material that will be more difficult to consult than when bound, and that will be at greater risk of damage through handling.

Post bindings are related to ring binders in that sheets are hole-punched and held in place on metal posts (see Figure 7.10). The posts can usually be dismantled allowing the sheets to be removed and then replaced after imaging so no further work is needed to rebind or rehouse the documents. Sometimes the posts can be unscrewed, either by hand or by using a screwdriver; other post bindings feature a mechanism that means they come

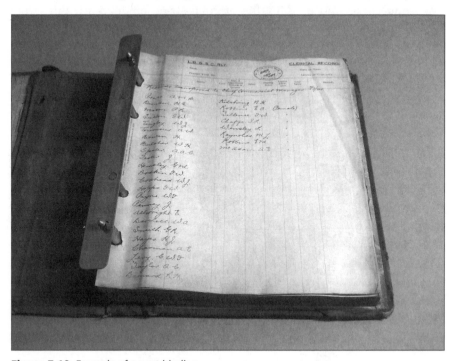

Figure 7.10 *Example of a post binding*

apart simply by pressing a lever. Dismantling a post binding can be done at the time of imaging by the operator and does not need the attention of a conservator. However, the resulting loose sheets can be more awkward to handle than bound sheets, particularly if they are damaged. Also, a post binding may not come apart if the mechanism is damaged or rusty, in which case it should be imaged with the binding in place.

Side sewing, also known as stab sewing, is a style of sewing where the string or thread is stitched through the entire thickness of the volume from front to back (see Figure 7.11). Often the sewing can be easily cut or untied and removed. Alternatively, if the string is long enough, it may be possible to untie and loosen it for imaging, tightening and retying the string afterwards. This is simply done and can be carried out by the operator. Removing or loosening the sewing may be unfeasible if the sewing is very tight or if glue has been used to secure the sheets. In this case a conservator should assess the binding to decide whether or not disbinding is advisable. If the sewing is removed it may be possible for a conservator to rebind the item using the existing sewing holes and cover, and possibly the original string or thread. If this is not feasible or is considered to be too time-consuming then the loose sheets should be rehoused in folders or paper wrappers.

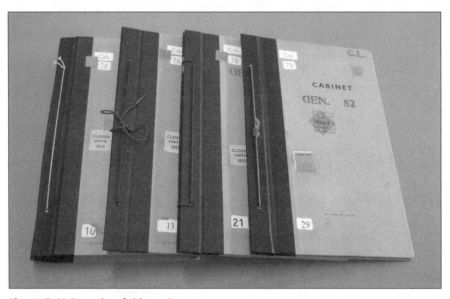

Figure 7.11 *Examples of side sewing*

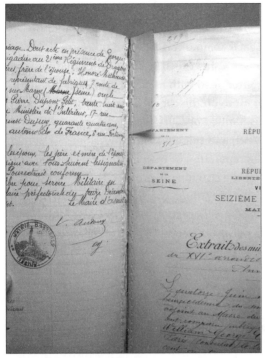

Oversewing is also known as library binding. Groups of loose sheets are sewn together in sections with small stitches (see Figure 7.12) done by hand or by machine. A bound volume is made up of several of these sections sewn together inside a case binding. Oversewing is particularly difficult to remove, not only because of the large number of stitches that need to be unpicked, but also because disbinding will necessitate the removal of the cover and spine lining. This must be done by a conservator and can be up to one day's work per item. As a further negative, when

Figure 7.12 *The oversewing stitches are small and numerous*

dismantling such a binding there is a strong risk of causing damage to the papers; the sheets will be perforated at their edge with many sewing holes, and thus be very fragile and prone to breakage. In some cases, the text beneath the sewing may not be legible once the sewing has been removed because the paper is so badly damaged. In general it is not advisable to attempt to remove oversewing unless the binding is already damaged.

When disbinding is appropriate

If a binding is easily removed and replaced, such as a post binding, then this can be incorporated into the workflow with minimal impact on the imaging operation. There may be other situations where disbinding is desirable and can be carried out without putting documents at risk. As with the removal of other fastenings, the rehousing or refastening of the resulting loose papers should be carefully considered.

CASE STUDY: 1911 census records

The records of the 1911 census of England and Wales were housed in more than 35,000 bound volumes with each volume consisting of up to several hundred sheets. A pilot project to test a sheet-feed scanner concluded that the sheets could be scanned via automated feed with minimal risk. (See Chapter 6 'Equipment for image capture' for more on the choice of scanner in this case study.) The volumes were easily dismantled because the sheets were held together with strings (see Figure 7.13) and there was no other adhesive or fastening used in the binding. The preparation of the volumes was carried out by scanning staff as the first step of the scanning operation. The strings were cut or untied and discarded. Staff leafed through the sheets correcting minor damage and removing pins and staples as necessary. If a sheet was found to be damaged it was inserted into a polyester sleeve. The loose sheets were kept within the original covers and tied with cotton ties (see Figure 7.14). It was essential to retain the original covers because they contained contextual information such as document reference numbers that was not on the individual documents. See Chapter 8 'Preparation of damaged documents' for more detail on how damaged documents were prepared in this case study.

After scanning, all polyester sleeves were removed and the items were boxed. Given the simple construction of the volumes, rebinding would have been possible and could have been carried out by the scanning team. However the original covers and the boxes provided good protection for the loose sheets, which were also held in place by the cotton ties. A major factor in the decision not to rebind was that the collection would remain in storage

Figure 7.13 *Census volume before scanning held together by two strings*

Figure 7.14 *After scanning the strings have been removed and the volume is secured with cotton ties*

once the digital surrogate was available and it was intended that the original documents would only be consulted under exceptional circumstances (Ahmon, 2008, 27). Also, if the originals were handled, the sequence would be maintained as all sheets were numbered.

The National Archives UK catalogue reference: RG 14 General Register Office:
1911 Census Schedules

Online at www.1911census.co.uk

Disbinding is appropriate if the existing binding is already severely damaged. In this situation the binding is no longer functioning properly; the cover is no longer protecting the pages; the binding is shedding debris; and/or the sewing is broken putting the papers under strain. The damaged binding may be removed and there may be justification for rebinding or rehousing the papers after imaging depending on their overall condition.

CASE STUDY: Judges' reports

This small collection of mixed papers consisted of letters and reports from judges concerning criminal cases from 1784 to 1830, many of which were held at the Old Bailey in London. The papers had been oversewn and bound into volumes. The majority of these volumes were severely damaged (see Figure 7.15) and had broken down into pieces. Rather than repair the original bindings, the volumes were disbound and the papers rehoused. This was a

Figure 7.15 *Judges' reports with damaged binding*

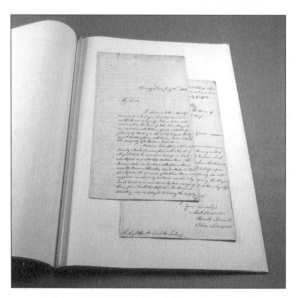

Figure 7.16 *Some of the documents from Figure 7.15 after disbinding and rehousing*

highly labour-intensive project that involved removing the cover from each volume then cutting and unpicking the sewing. Each document was then flattened before being mounted in specially made folios thus greatly facilitating the image capture (see Figure 7.16).

The National Archives UK catalogue reference: HO 47 Home Office: Judges' Reports on Criminals

Digitization in progress

Fitting preparation into the workflow

When considering how to fit preparation work into the workflow there are several factors to take into account.

• What preparation is needed?
• How long will the preparation take?
• Can the work be carried out by the imaging staff or does it need the attention of a conservator?
• Does every item require preparation or only some of the collection?

The collection survey has a vital role to play in underpinning the decision making when planning such an operation. See Chapter 5 'Surveying collections'.

To a large extent the question of who carries out the preparation is dictated by the nature of the preparation and what needs to be done. The majority of issues described in this chapter can be dealt with by the imaging operator (see Table 7.1 for a summary). In addition, the imaging operator will be able to deal with certain types of minor damage (see Table 8.1 in Chapter 8 'Preparation of damaged documents'). If conservation work to address damage is not required then there are two approaches to document preparation, outlined below. These options would also be valid if all conservation work is carried out separately ahead of imaging, or if the estimated amount of conservation is small enough to be dealt with using an *ad hoc* approach.

Option one: All preparation work carried out at imaging station

For a relatively small project involving less than 100 items where an imaging operator is responsible for all aspects of image capture, it may be sufficient for the operator to address the unpacking and preparation of documents as imaging progresses. This can be comfortably accommodated so long as the target image capture rate takes account of the total time needed from beginning to end. The operator may encounter issues that need the attention of a conservator but they can seek advice from the collection manager as these arise.

The operator should receive preservation training so as to ensure safe document handling, and the design of the scanning station should include sufficient work space for the operator to prepare the documents. This may be the only option if resources are limited. However, it may be inefficient and is not necessarily the best use of the operator's time, particularly if they are a skilled technician or professional photographer. The operator will already have demands on their time, having to deal with the equipment, image checking and metadata creation. So while this is the simplest approach, and gives complete control to the operator, it will result in a slower rate of image capture.

Option two: Preparation as a separate operation

For a larger project involving hundreds or thousands of items and numerous imaging staff, preparation of documents can be incorporated into the workflow as a separate operation before imaging. The advantage of this is that all documents are checked before going to the imaging station so that any problems are identified and dealt with in advance. This means that the imaging itself can proceed smoothly, thus avoiding a situation where the scanning operator needs to return an unfit item. In addition the operator can concentrate solely on operating the equipment to capture the best image because they can be confident that all items they receive are ready to scan.

Carrying out preparation separately from imaging adds complexity. The workflow must be carefully balanced so that there is a constant steady supply of prepared documents ready to be imaged and preparation does not cause a bottleneck in the operation. This option therefore works best for a large project where the documents are very similar, with each item requiring a small amount of preparation, and where damage is minor and is widely distributed throughout the collection.

Document preparation and conservation work

If a considerable proportion of the collection requires conservation work then it may be simplest for a conservator to carry out all preparation of documents including addressing formats and fastenings as well as all types of damage. As detailed in previous sections there are some preparation tasks that should only be done by a conservator, such as separation of glued items and some types of disbinding (see Table 7.1). There may be other tasks such as unfolding of bundles that would be preferably carried out by a conservator if items are fragile.

However, before opting for this approach it is worth considering if this is the most effective use of the conservator's time, especially if many of the tasks could easily be carried out by the imaging staff. Projects should be considered on a case-by-case basis because timescales and skill levels of staff will also be factors. It may be more efficient to integrate the conservation work into the imaging operation so that the conservator works alongside the imaging team. The options for this are discussed in Chapter 8 'Preparation of damaged documents'.

Chapter summary

- Preparing documents before imaging may require additional resources but it prevents avoidable delays during image capture and helps to ensure that good quality images are captured. The collection survey will indicate to what extent preparation is needed.
- Removal of fastenings should be carefully considered because this can be particularly time-consuming and has implications for the long-term preservation of the documents.
- Flattening of folded and rolled items can be carried out in advance to ensure that items will lie flat when imaged.
- Most disbinding would need to be carried out by a conservator. It will often result in unacceptable destruction of original material and may not be necessary if equipment can be adapted to deal with difficult bindings.
- Preparation can be carried out as a separate operation before imaging. This can be highly effective for a large, relatively consistent, collection.

Bibliography

Ahmon, J. (2008) Digitisation of 1911 census schedules, *ICON News: the magazine of the Institute of Conservation*, **14**, (January), 25–28.

Roberts, M. T. and Etherington, R. (1982) *Bookbinding and the Conservation of books: a dictionary of descriptive terminology*, Library of Congress, http://cool.conservation-us.org/don/don.html.

8

Preparation of damaged documents

Introduction

Preparing a collection for imaging as described in Chapter 7 'Preparation of document formats and fastenings' will help to ensure effective and efficient image capture. However, if items in a collection are damaged then this will also need to be addressed. Preparing damaged documents for image capture need not be a lengthy and expensive process. However, it will undoubtedly add to the costs of a project because, although it is not full conservation treatment, it should nevertheless be carried out by a qualified conservator. This makes it all the more important that the collection survey quantifies the amount of work needed so that an estimate of costs can be incorporated into the project budget at an early stage (see Chapter 5 'Surveying collections'). It is then possible to make informed decisions about whether or not a project conservator is needed and how conservation work might fit in with the imaging operation. This may need careful consideration because the nature of the preparation that is required may have an impact on the overall logistics.

Is conservation work always needed?

The short answer to this question is 'no' because the spot check and survey may suggest that there are no damaged items. In fact this may be one of the reasons why a particular collection was selected for digitization. However, if a proportion of the collection is found to be in fragile condition then these items can simply be excluded from the image capture, as discussed in Chapter 5 'Surveying collections'. If a full collection survey has been carried out then this will indicate which items should be excluded. If a sampled survey was carried out then an assessment stage to weed out unfit items may be needed during the imaging operation. However, if the imaging team are having to repeatedly reject items because they are unfit this is not a good use of their time and also unnecessarily uses resources for document ordering, tracking and delivery only to result in items being returned without being imaged. A full survey is therefore prefereable so that every item has been assessed in advance of the imaging.

If conservation work is not an option because there are no resources available then damaged items can be imaged in their current condition. If adopting this approach the institution must accept that not all information will be captured and the resulting digital image may be illegible. This may be undesireable if users are expected to pay to access the digital images online. There would also be a risk of causing further damage during the imaging of a fragile item. However, this approach can still aid the preservation of a vulnerable item by reducing the need to handle it in the near future.

Major and minor damage

Many common types of damage can be considered as minor and do not require conservation work. Minor damage can be corrected at the time of imaging by the operator. Examples of minor damage would be folded corners

and curled edges (see Figure 8.1) where the paper itself is in good condition. These can be flattened by hand. Minor damage may also include small tears, less than 5 cm in length, which do not affect the text. Major damage (see Figure 8.2) would be more severe in terms of quantity and extent. Such damage should receive the attention of a conservator and is not recommended for operators.

Figure 8.1 *Minor damage can be corrected by hand at the time of imaging*

The distinction between major and minor damage is not always clear-cut but Table 8.1 suggests

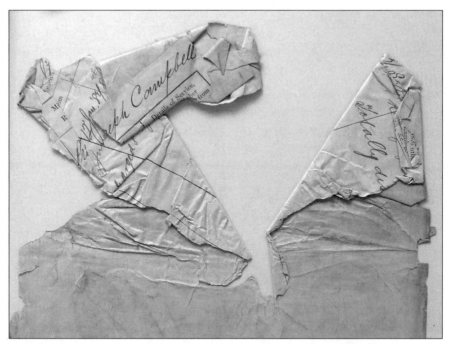

Figure 8.2 *More extensive damage requires the attention of a conservator*

Table 8.1 *Types of damage and who would deal with it*

	Operator	Conservator
Folds	✓	(if major damage)
Tears	✓	(if major damage)
Crumpled/curled sheet	✓	(if major damage)
Surface dirt	x	✓
Stuck pages	x	✓
Mould	x	✓
Previous repairs	x	✓

which types of damage are suitable for an operator and which would need to be seen by a conservator. In general, tasks that require the use of hand tools should be undertaken by a conservator because of the risk of causing damage to the document.

When assessing documents that are folded, torn or crumpled the overall stability of the document and the extent to which the text is affected should

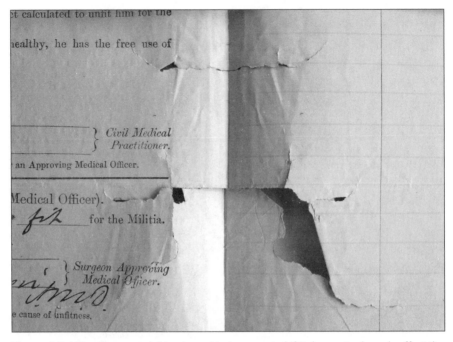

Figure 8.3 *Minor damage might not need to be corrected if it does not adversely affect the text or the stability of the document*

also be considered. For example, if a document has a large tear but the text is not affected (see Figure 8.3) and it can be imaged if handled with care then treatment will not be necessary. Similarly, if a damaged document is brittle or generally fragile (see Figure 8.4) then flattening would be best carried out by a conservator because of the risk of causing further damage.

The skills of the operator should also be taken into consideration. Preservation training and written guidelines can help operators recognize damage and judge whether or not a conservator is needed. With experience an operator can tell if an item is safe to handle and be imaged, and with time they will gain the confidence to handle minor damage themselves.

Use of conservation technicians

Ideally, preparation of items with major damage should be carried out by a project conservator, for the reasons discussed in Chapter 2 'Before you digitize: resources, suppliers and surrogates'. However, for some projects it

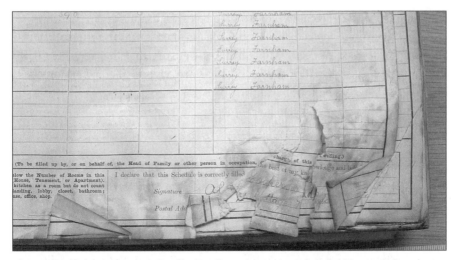

Figure 8.4 *If the document is fragile then flattening and repair should be carried out by a conservator*

may not be possible for a conservator to carry out all of the preparation work, for example, if there are insufficient funds or if conservators are fully committed to other projects. In such a situation an acceptable compromise would be for the work to be carried out by a skilled conservation technician or conservation assistant under the supervision of a conservator so that the conservator is then available for other duties. The conservation work involves a minimal amount of treatment – just enough to facilitate the imaging and no more – and if a conservator is available to manage the work and make treatment decisions then the actual treatments can be carried out by a technician or assistant. This would still need to be someone with experience of carrying out paper repairs and basic treatments, and would not be suitable work for someone without this previous experience.

Treatment options

The conservation work to prepare major damage for imaging would typically involve repair, flattening, cleaning, separating stuck sheets, removal of old repairs and mould cleaning. As discussed in Chapter 7 'Preparation of document formats and fastenings', it may also include removal of restrictive fastenings or damaged housings. Lastly, the item may need to be rehoused if fastenings have been removed or if items have been unfolded.

When deciding on treatment options, the conservator must take into account the context of digitization and must ensure that the treatment suits the aims of the digitization project. There are several factors to consider: document stability, legibility and time constraints.

Document stability

When aiming to stabilize a document the conservator must consider how the document will be processed during imaging. It is therefore helpful for them to know what equipment will be used. For example, unfolding may be the priority if using an overhead system that does not include a glass plate. It may also be relevant to know the level of skills and experience of the imaging team; a more experienced team will be more confident with handling difficult items. Conservation work to stabilize a document for imaging must be balanced with the anticipated reduction in handling once the digital images are available online.

Legibility

The conservator will prioritize items where the text is affected by damage. Even minor damage can make it difficult to read text, such as the obscured names in Figure 8.1. Tears and creases can cause words to be misaligned. Severe dirt can obscure text, as can past repairs, especially if the repair material and adhesive have aged badly. However, damage that does not affect the text might not need to be treated. With this in mind it quickly becomes apparent that not all damage needs treatment. An exception to this is that items that are affected by mould should be treated before they can be handled regardless of whether or not text is affected. Also, it may be necessary to treat items that have no text just enough so that the user can see that there is no text there.

Time constraints

It is highly likely that the conservator will be under pressure to complete a large quantity of treatments within a given timescale. This is because a project may require the treatment of hundreds of items and since the conservation work is usually the first part of the process if there are delays at this stage then this may cause delays in the rest of the imaging schedule. It is therefore essential that the collection survey provides an accurate estimate of the time needed to carry out the conservation work. Table 8.2 indicates what work can be realistically carried out within given times. This uses the system of damage codes suggested in Chapter 5 'Surveying collections' (Table 5.3) and can be applied to a single bound volume or a box of loose papers. If specific problems are identified during the spot check assessment then it may be appropriate to carry out tests to explore treatment options and gauge how long treatment may take. This in turn will inform the survey so that time estimates are realistic.

In practice, preparation times can be reduced by keeping treatments to a minimum, by avoiding the use of moisture and solvents (since wet treatments will require drying time), and by working in batches so that several items are treated at the same time. The conservator may decide to prioritize the worst affected items while deciding not to treat those that are damaged but still legible.

When stability, legibility and time constraints are taken into consideration

Table 8.2 Damage codes and treatments		
Damage code	**Estimated preparation time**	**Extent of treatment**
Code 0	no preparation needed	Document ready to scan, no preparation needed. Minor damage only.
Code 1	up to 30 minutes	Flattening of a few curled or folded edges. One repair.
Code 2	up to one hour	Flattening of curled or folded edges. A few repairs. Small amount of mould cleaning.
Code 3	up to 3 hours (half a day)	Same type of damage as code 2, but greater quantity. Rehousing possibly needed. Extensive mould cleaning.
Code 4	up to 6 hours (whole day)	Same type of damage as code 3, but greater quantity. Document with specific problem where more extensive treatment must be considered, for example, crumpled parchment.

 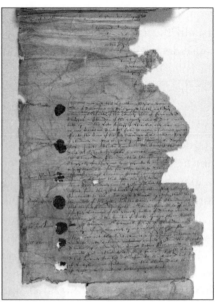

Figure 8.5 *Fragile paper document with major damage*

Figure 8.6 *The document from Figure 8.5 prepared for imaging by a conservator*

it becomes clear that some conservation treatments might not be appropriate for the digitization context, for example, repairs to bindings, loss compensation or consolidation. These are treatments that may result in a significant improvement to the stability of a document but not necessarily to its legibility. Also such treatments can be very time-consuming and so might not be suitable when many documents are in need of treatment within a tight timescale.

Figures 8.5 and 8.6 illustrate how an item prepared for imaging by a conservator may look before and after treatment. In this example, the document was gently unfolded and relaxed under boards and weights. No moisture was used during this process. The weakest torn areas were supported with small minimal repairs. Due to its fragility the item was rehoused in a folder. No loss compensation was carried out and the document was not lined or resized.

Options for severely damaged items

In some situations there is little that a conservator can do to stabilize an item other than lengthy conservation treatment, for example, if paper is fragmented or has suffered large areas of loss. One option would be to omit such items from the imaging but, as already mentioned, this may be undesirable because it will result in gaps in the digital surrogate. Another option is to carry out a minimal treatment and then insert the item into a transparent sleeve to provide support. Polyester serves this purpose well because it is strong, colourless, crystal clear and is relatively rigid. The static between the two sides also helps to keep the item flat and prevents it moving inside the sleeve.

Polyester sheets are made in different thicknesses but for most items 75 microns is thick enough to provide protection and support, even for items up to A2 in size. The size of the polyester sleeve will be dictated by the size of the documents it shall be holding, and possibly the size of the bed of the imaging equipment that shall be being used, but size will also be determined by the design of the sleeve and its main purpose; for example, if it is a priority for the sleeve to hold the item flat then it will help if the sleeve is oversized. The sleeve can be designed to be open on one, two or three edges; a sleeve welded on all four edges, totally encapsulating the item, is only appropriate if the sleeve is intended for permanent storage.

A sleeve which is open on only one edge (so welded on three edges) will provide the best security for the item because it is less likely to move inside the sleeve or fall out. However, it can be awkward to insert (and later remove) the item from the sleeve, particularly if it is a tight fit. By contrast a sleeve with only one welded edge will open up to allow for the quick and easy insertion of an item that needs to be positioned carefully, but the sleeve may not provide sufficient support. A sleeve with two welded and two open edges may be a good compromise, offering a degree of rigidity and support but also easy access (see Figure 8.7).

If many documents are inserted into sleeves this can add considerably to the overall bulk of an item that, as a result, may no longer fit back into its housing or box. This is a consideration when fitting preparation of damaged documents into the workflow, as discussed later. After image capture the sleeves can be removed and re-used, although if they have been used for mould-affected items they should not be re-used because of the risk of contaminating other documents. The removal of sleeves will require an additional stage in the imaging operation. An alternative option is to leave

Figure 8.7 *Polyester sleeve welded on two edges*

the polyester sleeves *in situ* to serve as protective storage, so long as the increased bulk is not a problem. If considering this option then it is important to consult a conservator because polyester is not an appropriate storage material for some types of document and under certain storage conditions.

Despite its many advantages, the polyester sleeve is an additional expense. Polyester is also easily scratched and so sleeves can only be used a few times before they must be discarded. A more significant issue is that the shiny surface of the polyester can cause glare in the digital image. This is not always a problem, but if considering using polyester sleeves they should be tested to see if the resulting images are acceptable. Polypropylene is an alternative material that may not reflect light as much as polyester and may be cheaper; however, polypropylene is neither as rigid nor as clear, having a slightly textured surface that may interfere with the clarity of the digital image.

Sleeving works well for loose sheets but may not be practical for bound items and some fastened items. Also, polyester sleeves would not be suitable for friable materials such as unconsolidated brittle and mould-affected paper because the static between the polyester sheets may cause damage. For such items it would still be feasible to digitize if the handling can be done by a conservator or with the assistance of a conservator. The handling can be facilitated by interleaving (see Figure 8.8). This is when a sheet of paper is inserted behind each damaged sheet. During imaging the supporting paper is handled rather than the damaged document. The interleaving sheets can be removed after imaging. This may be a slow process but it should result in successful image capture that will enhance access to otherwise inaccessible items.

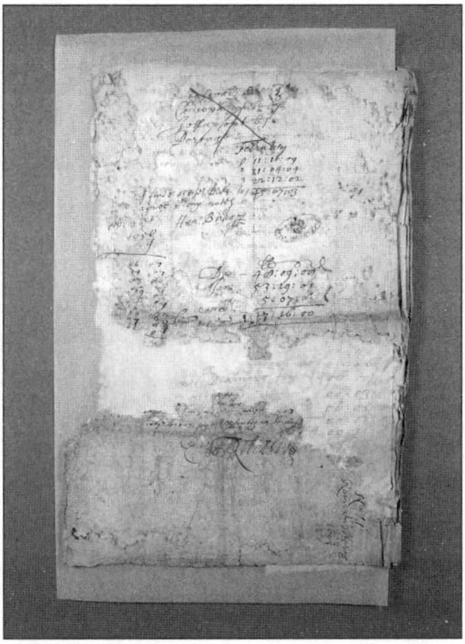

Documentation

If conservation work is carried out on a collection then this should be documented. An institution may

Figure 8.8 *Interleaving can be used to provide additional support to very weak sheets*

already have a system in place for such documentation. If not, then all that is needed is a generic description of the treatments that were conducted and the date, since it is unlikely that a digitization project would include full technical examination and analysis. It is also useful to record the time taken.

As with all projects, it is important to monitor the progress of the conservation work so as to ensure that work is on track and will be completed on time. This is particularly important if the conservation work is on a tight schedule and may hold up the scanning if it falls behind. Monthly progress reports are useful for tracking progress. These need not be long reports because all that is needed is a log of the number of items treated and time taken. It is also useful to maintain statistics on progress, for example, percentage of items treated thus far. This is a good way to identify milestones such as the treatment of 2000 boxes.

On conclusion of the project it is worth analysing the data to calculate average treatment time, and to see if estimates were accurate or not. This is an opportunity to ask what went well and what did not go well and what would be done differently next time. This 'lessons learned' exercise is part of good practice in project management because it will inform future projects. This data analysis is much easier if records are consistently maintained throughout the project.

Fitting conservation work into the workflow

There are different ways in which conservation work can be incorporated into the workflow of the imaging operation. Factors to consider when deciding how to approach this are listed below.

- *Extent of conservation work.* What proportion of the collection is in need of conservation work and how these items are distributed in the collection.
- *Nature of the treatment.* Some conservation work may need to be carried out in a conservation studio. If polyester sleeves are used then it may not be possible to repack items and return them to the store (due to the added bulk).
- *Physical nature of documents.* Documents may be difficult to transport if they are particularly large or heavy.
- *Duration of the project.* For projects involving the imaging of thousands of items the workflow must be designed so as to be efficient but also robust and sustainable over the long term.
- *Size of the project.* The workflow may involve transferring documents between imaging and conservation teams. This may be logistically difficult for large quantities.

Logistics and resources feature heavily in this list and may be the deciding factors if there is simply not enough space to house a conservator alongside the imaging team or if the conservation studio cannot accommodate a digitization project. An image capture operation can involve the bulk transport, storage, tracking and processing of large quantities of documents and so must be carefully managed. It is wise to aim for the simplest solutions.

Three options are suggested here. These vary in the degree to which the conservation work is embedded in the imaging operation. In option one the conservation work and imaging are separate operations. In options two and three the conservation work is integrated with the imaging, either working in advance of the imaging (option two) or reactively (option three).

Option 1: Conservation as a separate operation

The preparation of damaged documents can be carried out as a completely separate operation thereby ensuring that the entire collection is ready to be scanned before the imaging starts. Work can be carried out in the conservation studio where all the necessary tools, equipment and materials are to hand. It works best for documents that can be easily repacked for delivery to the imaging team once they have been prepared; for example, if damaged items are inserted into polyester sleeves they may no longer fit inside their boxes so alternative arrangements would be needed such as rehousing.

Option one is preferable for many reasons, not least the peace of mind of those who are managing the image capture. They can rest assured that the entire collection has already been assessed by a conservator and major damage has been prepared as necessary. The imaging team may still need to deal with some minor damage and document preparation but anything needing the attention of a conservator will have been already addressed. This is also the simplest way of organizing the workflow – once the conservator has finished preparing the collection the imaging can commence and there is no need for complex scheduling to co-ordinate the activities of the conservation and imaging teams.

This approach works well if a full survey has been carried out so the conservation work has been quantified in full and all items in need of preparation have been identified. If a sample has been surveyed then the rest of the collection will need to be assessed so as to identify which items are in need of preparation. The time needed to carry out this assessment should be included in the estimated time needed for preparation. This would not be needed if the survey found that every item in the collection required preparation.

It is important to recognize that adhering to the time estimates becomes critical because if the preparation takes significantly longer than anticipated this will have a knock-on effect on the rest of the operation and then on all subsequent phases of the project. If operating within a tight timescale it should still be possible to meet deadlines by increasing the available resource, for example by halving the time needed by doubling the workforce.

Time pressures may make this option unfeasible for many projects because of the need for a lead-in time before imaging can start. Very large projects can entail months or even years of a conservator's time due to the volume of work and it may not be possible to wait for the preparation of damaged documents to finish before imaging starts. Even once the preparation is completed it is still advisable for a conservator to be available so as to advise on handling issues or carry out remedial work that may have been missed by the collection survey.

CASE STUDY: 1911 census records

The project to digitize census forms from the 1911 census of England and Wales involved scanning more than 35,000 bound volumes. A collection survey was carried out at an early stage, looking at the condition of a sample of just over 400 books. Results indicated that minor damage was widespread throughout the collection, but also that only a tiny percentage of volumes had major damage and would require conservation work. Typical problems needing preparation by a conservator included mould damage, stuck pages and severe edge damage. A concurrent relabelling project was the ideal opportunity to identify the volumes in need of conservation work so the relabelling project team were asked to record the references of volumes with major damage. They received training from conservators to help them recognize different types of damage.

A pilot project was set up to prepare 200 of the damaged volumes for scanning. This showed that the average treatment time was two hours per volume. On the basis of the pilot project it was possible to estimate the time, cost and materials needed to complete all of the conservation work. Due to the scale of the scanning operation there was a considerable lead-in time before scanning started, providing a generous window of opportunity to complete the preparation of damaged documents. In total 1108 volumes were treated by a team of project conservators over 485 person-days (Ahmon, 2008, 27) .

All preparation was completed before scanning started. However, there remained a strong possibility that major damage would be encountered during the scanning operation. This is because the relabelling team only assessed the exterior of the volumes and did not open them up. Once scanning started, any volumes found to have major damage were set aside for conservation work. This work had to be carried out as soon as possible so as to minimize disruption to the scanning schedule. This meant that conservation staff were available at all times in case immediate treatment was needed. A further 190 volumes were treated in this way.

All minor damage was addressed by the scanning operators who received training from conservation staff on how to deal with different types of damage.

(See Chapter 6 'Equipment for image capture' for more on the choice of scanner in this case study and Chapter 7 'Preparation of document formats and fastenings' for more on the preparation of documents.)

The National Archives UK catalogue reference: RG 14 General Register Office: 1911 Census Schedules

Online at www.1911census.co.uk

If there is a tight timescale then any items which do not require preparation (i.e. items with damage code 0) can be made available for imaging immediately, thus scanning can start while the preparation of other documents is being completed. This would probably mean that items would thus not be imaged in sequence, although it is possible to schedule the operation in phases so that, if necessary, the conservator has a deadline for the preparation of a specific batch. This scheduling needs to be done with care and with ongoing communication between the preparation and imaging teams so that progress can be tracked by both sides. In practice this can become very complicated and it is all too easy for the conservation work to become a bottleneck in the workflow if the image capture out-paces it.

CASE STUDY: State Papers Online project

The State Papers Online (1509–1714) was a project involving the digitization of state papers covering more than 200 years of British history. The spot check assessment indicated that there was a range of formats and material including some badly damaged items and documents damaged by mould. A sampled survey was carried out and, based on the estimated time needed for the conservation work, a project conservator was employed. All work was carried out in the conservation studio but had to be carefully co-ordinated with the imaging team so that there was a steady supply of documents ready to image.

Since a sample of the documents had been assessed during the survey, one of the project conservator's first tasks was the assessment of the remainder of the documents. The timescale for this project was tight and so it was necessary for the imaging team to start work as soon as possible. The condition assessment provided a full list of all items that were ready to scan so the imaging was able to start and for the duration of the project the imaging was carried out concurrently with the conservation work, although as separate work streams.

The project shared documentation in the form of a spreadsheet, which the project conservator regularly updated as items were prepared. The imaging manager could then check to see which items were ready to be scanned. As the conservation work progressed, it was found that weekly meetings between the project conservator and the imaging manager were essential in order to maintain communication. For example, when the scanning team planned to increase through-put by bringing in extra staff the resource for conservation work was also increased so as to keep pace.

Particular problems were encountered with mould-damaged documents that required far more treatment than was originally estimated. This was addressed to some extent by rehousing, such as interleaving sheets to assist handling of weak pages. A few boxes of folded parchment membranes were also problematic because these needed to be unfolded and relaxed and once this was done they could not be boxed for transit to the imaging area. These parchments were taken from the conservation studio to the imaging team by the project conservator, were imaged immediately and then brought back to the studio and housed by the conservator. This was considered acceptable for a relatively small quantity of documents, but for a larger quantity a more robust solution would have been needed. A fuller account of the conservation work on this project is given by Ahmon, Baum and Brookes (2010).

The National Archives UK catalogue reference: SP series (various): State Paper Office: State Papers Domestic; State Papers Foreign, Ireland, Scotland, Borders and registers of the Privy Council
Online at http://gale.cengage.co.uk/state-papers-online-15091714.aspx

Option 2: Integrated with scanning operation

The conservation work can be carried out alongside the imaging operation so that they share the same workspace. The advantage of this is not only the face-to-face communication, but also that the conservator is on hand to assist immediately with any *ad hoc* queries or problems that arise as image capture progresses. The other advantage is that document tracking is simplified and there is no longer the need to physically move documents between different departments. This is particularly important for items which no longer fit inside their housings once they have been prepared, such as those that have been inserted into polyester sleeves, or folded items which must remain flat for imaging. It is preferable to minimize the time that documents are outside their housings as these protect them from accidents and hazards such as light exposure. These risks are minimized if such items can proceed directly to the operator for digitization and can then be safely repacked immediately afterwards.

Setting up a space for conservation work will mean providing suitable work surfaces, storage areas, lighting, equipment, materials and tools. It should not be added on as an after-thought. There may still be occasional tasks that must be carried out in a conservation studio. If the majority of documents require work that must be done in a conservation studio then it may be appropriate to set up the imaging operation in the studio itself.

The workflow will still need to be carefully managed so that the conservation keeps pace with the imaging and there is always a constant supply of prepared items. One way to manage the workflow is to divide the collection into batches, for example weekly deliveries. There will therefore always be a finite quantity of items to be checked and prepared within the week. For projects involving hundreds or thousands of items this may be easier than attempting to track individual items from end to end. The resources for conservation must match the resources for imaging so that the two operations can keep pace with one another. It is therefore critical to have a thorough understanding of the quantity and distribution of damaged items and the estimated time needed to prepare them for imaging. The collection survey will provide this information (see Chapter 5 'Surveying collections').

Option two would work well for a project where the majority of items require some preparation, but only quick, minimal work. This would make effective use of the conservator's time. Problems arise if individual items require more extensive work because of the degree of damage. There is a risk that the conservator may fall behind schedule so that the conservation and image capture become out of synch. This can be resolved by removing the problem item from the batch and imaging it later, so long as the operation can track items out of sequence.

CASE STUDY: Departures passenger lists

The departures passenger lists record passengers departing on ships at major UK ports from 1890 to 1960. The documents are very similar to the arrivals passenger lists as described in the case study in Chapter 7 'Preparation of document formats and fastenings'. The two projects to digitize the arrivals and departures passenger lists were carried out at The National Archives UK by two different commercial partners and so the imaging operations were run quite differently.

The imaging operation for the departures passenger lists consisted of three teams to carry out document preparation, conservation work and scanning. All three teams were situated in the same work area. The preparation team checked each box of documents and compiled a 'manifest' so that the scanning team would know the exact quantity of documents in each box and how they were arranged. This enabled them to prepare some of the metadata in advance of image capture. The preparation team also assessed the condition of the documents, assigning a damage code to each box so as to identify boxes containing documents in need of preparation by a conservator. The scanning schedule was divided into weekly batches and every week the manifest was updated and shared between the teams. The conservation team aimed to work a week ahead of the scanning team so that all documents were prepared the week before being delivered to the scanning team.

Having all three stages of the imaging operation situated in the same work area facilitated communication between the teams so that any difficulties with the workflow could be addressed immediately. It also meant that there was always a project conservator on hand to advise if either the preparation or scanning teams had queries. Batches of boxes passed from one team to another within a relatively short timespan. This was important because the departures passenger lists were a popular collection and so it was necessary to minimize the time that they would be unavailable to users of the reading room. The logistics of transferring boxes of documents between the teams was also simpler and easier than having to transport boxes around the building and so locating the teams together helped the operation run more efficiently.

The conservators used polyester sleeves so that documents with major damage could be stabilized with the minimum of treatment. Once inserted into a sleeve, a document would no longer fit inside its box and so was left outside the box until after imaging. While outside its box the document was at risk of becoming lost or disassociated. However, this risk was accepted because there was a relatively short time between conservation and scanning and because the documents would not need to leave the work area during this time. As soon as the sleeved document had been imaged the polyester sleeve was removed to be re-used and the document could then be repacked in its box.

The National Archives UK catalogue reference: BT 27 Board of Trade: Commercial and Statistical Departments and Successors: Outwards Passenger Lists

Online at www.ancestorsonboard.com

Option 3: Working reactively within scanning operation

The conservator can work in a reactive way, treating items as they are flagged up by the imaging team. All items go straight to the imaging operators and are only referred to the conservator as necessary. After an item has been treated by the conservator it is returned to the operator for re-scans. This means that there is no risk of the conservation work causing a bottleneck in the operation and the operators will not run out of work. This option also has all the advantages of having a conservator embedded in the imaging operation, and makes effective use of their time because they will only treat items that the operators cannot image.

The main disadvantage of this approach is that it is dependent on the imaging team to identify documents in need of conservation work. There is a risk that the operators flag up large quantities of minor damage and thus overload the conservator with unnecessary work, or else they image damaged items without flagging them up, resulting in unreadable images. This can be addressed by training and ongoing support which can be provided by the on-site conservator.

This option is best suited to collections where the majority of items are undamaged and ready to scan. It works particularly well for loose document formats where there may be a large quantity of material per box that is not easy to assess (see Case study: Soldiers' service records) and it also reduces unnecessary handling because items that do not require preparation are handled only once, when they are scanned. As with option two, the conservation resource needs to be carefully balanced with the resource for imaging so that the operation runs smoothly over the long term.

CASE STUDY: Soldiers' service records

The project to digitize British soldiers' records from the period 1760 to 1913 involved imaging more than three million loose sheets housed in more than 6000 boxes. Each box contained up to 200 records, each of which consisted of several loose sheets – an estimated 1000 images per box. The survey showed that around 40% of the boxes contained badly damaged documents in need of preparation by a conservator, but that typically only up to three documents in each of these boxes required such work. Given the huge quantity of documents in each box the task of identifying the major damage would take as long as the actual treatment. This problem was encountered during the survey, when it took up to 45 minutes to assess the overall condition of a box by leafing through the contents.

Given the wide distribution of such a small number of damaged documents it was decided that the project conservator should work alongside the imaging team and treat damaged documents as they encountered them during the imaging. The workflow was simple: if the operator could not image a particular document they took an image to serve as a dummy digital file, then inserted a marker sheet and continued with the imaging. When they finished imaging a box, if conservation work was needed then it was passed to the conservator. When the conservation work was completed, the box was returned to the operator who then took re-scans of the treated items and removed the marked sheets.

Ten camera stations were set up, processing 20 boxes a day, and the project ran smoothly with the support of only one project conservator post (run as a job share). The workload fluctuated, and at times, when there were no boxes in their 'in tray', the conservators occupied themselves by carrying out preparation work on unscanned boxes. There were busy times when a backlog of conservation work accumulated but this did not cause a problem with the workflow. The imaging team did not run out of work because there was a steady supply of boxes to be imaged. On conclusion it was found that just under 40% of boxes received treatment from the conservator, who treated an average of seven boxes a day. The project conservator post was run as a job share so as to reduce the impact of absence due to leave or sickness. Both conservators adapted their methodology to treat documents in batches so as to cope with the volume of work generated by the camera team.

The use of marker sheets reduced handling because only those marked by the operator were treated and re-scanned. Document handling overall was reduced because all of the documents in good condition or with only minor damage were handled once, during imaging. All camera operators received training from the project conservator in document handling and were also trained to recognize when conservation work was needed. Judgements as to what constitutes major damage can vary between individuals but the project conservator was working physically adjacent to the imaging team so was always available for occasional queries.

The National Archives UK catalogue reference: WO 97 Royal Hospital Chelsea: Soldiers' Service Documents

Online at www.findmypast.co.uk/MilitaryStartSearch.jsp

Chapter summary

- Minor damage can be corrected by the imaging team, but major damage must be prepared by a conservator, or conservation technicians or assistants under the supervision of a conservator.
- The preparation of damaged items aims to stabilize items for handling and ensure legibility. Also, it often must be completed within tight time constraints. These factors affect the way a conservator will approach treatment. Preparation for image capture is not full conservation treatment.
- Polyester sleeves can be used to protect very fragile items removing the need for lengthy conservation treatment. Alternatively, such items can be handled by a conservator at the time of imaging.
- There are a few different ways in which conservation work can be incorporated into the imaging operation. The approach to this will be determined by the results of the collection survey, which will indicate how much work is needed, the nature of the damage and how it is distributed.
- It may be appropriate to carry out a pilot project, or small scale tests, before

the collection survey so that treatment methodology can be defined. This will help to ensure that estimated times are realistic.

Bibliography

Ahmon, J. (2008) Digitisation of 1911 Census Schedules, *ICON News: the magazine of the Institute of Conservation*, **14** (January), 25–28.

Ahmon, J., Baum, C. and Brookes, A. (2010) State Papers Online, *ICON News: the magazine of the Institute of Conservation*, **30** (September), 16–18.

9

Setting up the imaging operation

Introduction

Document preparation as described in Chapter 7 'Preparation of document, formats and fastenings' and Chapter 8 'Preparation of damaged documents' is an indispensable part of an imaging operation not only to obtain the best possible image, but also for the sake of document welfare. However, there are numerous other aspects of the image capture operation that will have a bearing on document welfare. The use of original documents in a reading room would usually be subject to many restrictions and, similarly, imaging should be carried out in controlled conditions. Activities such as cleaning of equipment or use of marker sheets are seemingly minor but do have preservation implications. The collection manager should therefore be involved during the planning and setting up of the imaging operation so that they can advise on these issues.

A large-scale operation can involve hundreds if not thousands of documents and a team of project staff working to a tight timescale. A poorly designed operation is potentially inefficient but also poses the risk of accidents to documents or staff, or the risk of items becoming mislaid or out of sequence. The operation should therefore take account of the processing and imaging requirements, and the preservation requirements of the documents, and balance this with the comfort and safety of the project staff.

Working environment

The choice of working on-site or off-site has been discussed in Chapter 2 'Before you digitize: resources, suppliers and surrogates'. From a preservation perspective an on-site operation is preferable because it will utilize existing systems, for example systems for document ordering, delivery and security, and because the transport of items to an off-site location poses a fresh set of risks. However, the factor that is common to both off-site and on-site operations is the need for appropriate environmental conditions.

When establishing requirements for environmental conditions the institution should balance the needs of the collection with the needs of the imaging operation, in particular the need for human comfort. Documents will only be in the imaging area for a few weeks at a time and so there is scope for some flexibility in environmental requirements. It is always advisable to monitor the temperature and humidity in the workspace because the environmental conditions are likely to change once furniture, equipment, people and documents are in place and imaging gets underway. If equipment and lighting are found to generate much heat then adequate ventilation should help to prevent this building up.

As discussed in Chapter 6 'Equipment for image capture', bright lighting poses a relatively low risk to documents. However, it may be a source of discomfort for the operators who will be exposed to the lights for longer than the documents will. Once equipment is set up it may be necessary to ensure that lights are shaded so that staff are not dazzled, especially the operators who will be required to work in close proximity to the lights. In general it is good practice to keep ambient light levels to a minimum, so ideally the imaging operation should be set up in an area without windows. If ambient light levels are low then it is important to remove trip hazards from the work area, such as bags, coats and trailing wires.

Ambient light may interfere with the image capture equipment and light sources can cause reflections on monitor screens. Similarly sources of bright colours such as signage can interfere with image capture by causing reflections and so should be covered (Frey and Reilly, 2006, 32). Monitors should be positioned so that such reflections are not a problem. Ideally the work area should be painted with grey walls and a black ceiling (Palm, 2010). This is particularly important if accurate colour rendering is a priority as it provides good conditions for viewing the digital images on screen.

Size and layout of the workspace

The workspace should be large enough to accommodate all elements of the imaging operation. Requirements will be dictated largely by the size of the equipment and furniture but the design of the workflow will also be a consideration. For example, it may be necessary to include a separate area for document preparation by the imaging team, and yet another area for conservation work. The workspace should also include sufficient storage space for documents. The document storage should be arranged so that it is easy to distinguish between items awaiting imaging, items for conservation, items to be returned, and so on. It may be appropriate for the different teams (preparation, conservation and imaging) to have separate document storage areas near to their work areas.

A well designed workspace will greatly facilitate the smooth running of an imaging operation. This will not only help to ensure efficiency, but also if staff can work comfortably then they will be able to concentrate on their work and will be less prone to mistakes and accidents. The layout of the area should reflect the workflow of the operation so that documents progress from one area to the next in a logical sequence. Ideally, imaging stations should be physically separate so as to reduce the risk of documents getting mixed up, or losing sequence or associations.

The imaging station

It is easy to underestimate the amount of work surface and storage space needed for an imaging operation, both in the workspace as a whole and at each individual imaging station. A typical imaging station will need to accommodate:

- the unpacking and repacking of items
- storage of packing materials
- scanned and unscanned items
- imaging equipment (scanner or camera stand, PC, monitor, keyboard)
- small items such as paperclips, a pencil, notepaper, marker sheets and personal effects
- cleaning materials.

The storage of packing materials is particularly significant if it is the housing rather than the item that is marked with the document reference. If this is the case then it is imperative that items are reunited with their correct housings after imaging. An item which is returned to the wrong box is as good as lost.

During imaging, documents should always be fully supported on the work surface, not be overhanging the edge or perched on the operator's lap, and never placed on a chair or on the floor. When imaging loose papers it is important that the operator can stack scanned and unscanned items in

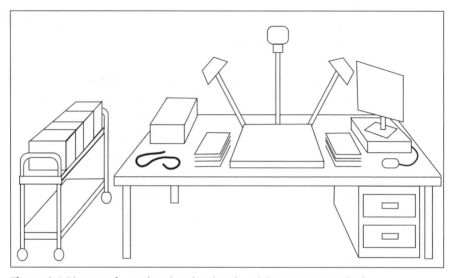

Figure 9.1 *Diagram of a workstation showing the minimum space required*

separate piles so that they can keep track of their work and keep items in the correct sequence. As a basic guideline the work surface should be six times the size of the original document (Library of Congress, 1999). Figure 9.1 shows that this is a minimum requirement and once everything is taken into account the required work surface area is in fact much larger.

All furniture should be fit for purpose in that it should provide a comfortable working environment while ensuring sufficient work surfaces and storage for the documents, packing materials and all equipment. Desks and chairs should be at a suitable height so that staff can work comfortably and can handle the documents safely. Trolleys are a useful addition to the work area and may be necessary for health and safety reasons if documents are particularly large or heavy. Documents should not be stored on trolleys but trolleys can be used for temporary storage of housing materials.

Health and safety

In most countries there are minimum requirements for health and safety in the workplace as laid down in legislation. For an imaging operation the main risks are likely to be from:

- repetitive actions if furniture and equipment is not in a comfortable working position
- manual handling if staff repeatedly lift and handle very heavy items
- eye strain from use of display screens or the presence of very bright light sources
- trips and falls, particularly if low light levels are maintained and the workplace is over-crowded with equipment, trailing cables, staff and furniture.

Legislation may also include guidelines as to what is an agreeable temperature for human comfort. This issue may arise if equipment is emitting heat and the workspace is poorly ventilated.

A health and safety inspection would typically involve a risk assessment of the workplace followed by implementation of preventive measures to control the risks but really these issues should be considered from the outset so as to create a safe, healthy environment for the imaging operation. This will not only ensure the welfare of staff but will also contribute to document welfare since accidents are less likely to occur in a healthy workplace.

There should be no food and drink in the area where original documents are stored or used due to the risk of damage from a spillage. It may therefore be necessary to provide a separate area for staff breaks. Ideally, the workspace should also be free of bags and coats. This is partially for security reasons as smaller items may be susceptible to pilfering, but is also a health and safety precaution as bags and coats can be a trip hazard. This issue can be addressed by providing lockers for staff.

Tools and materials

The use of tools and materials in the work area should be restricted in line with the restrictions in a reading room or any other area where original documents are used. This will include the exclusion of pens in favour of pencils, and the exclusion of document-altering stationery items such as scissors, staplers, adhesive tape and correcting fluid. The imaging process should not involve adding material to the original documents such as adhesive labels or barcodes; however, these can be used in the form of marker sheets that can be removed after imaging. If marker sheets are used, a paper should be chosen that is in contrast to the original documents so that it is easily identified and removed at the end; for example, an oversized sheet can be used. However, brightly coloured paper should be avoided, as their dyes are usually neither lightfast nor waterproof and may cause staining of originals should they remain in the box. Other ways of signifying a marker sheet is to include on it the institution's or company's logo and the date so that it is clearly identifiable as not being part of the original document.

Cleaning and maintenance

The cleaning of a workspace is an essential element of good housekeeping and may be required on a daily basis, particularly if documents are shedding dirt and debris. Very fine dust may be particularly problematic as it will easily transfer onto hands, clothes and other documents and once airborne will settle on equipment and work surfaces. Dirt and debris can appear in the digital images but may also scratch glass plates and can cause problems with electrical equipment. This can lead to downtime while maintenance and cleaning of equipment is carried out. Dust may also cause health problems if it is fine enough to be inhaled. Staff who are particularly sensitive to this should be advised to wear a mask.

Cleaning should always be carried out towards the end of a shift after documents have been packed away. Use of wet cleaning products should be avoided due to the risk of spillage, and bottled fluids should not be stored in the same area where documents are stored for the same reason. Check that work surfaces and equipment are dry before starting work with original documents.

A range of products are available for cleaning computer and photographic equipment and most of these will be appropriate for an imaging station. In most cases dry cleaning will be sufficient, such as wiping with a dry microfibre cloth. Pressurized air from a canister will also work well, as will a blower, available from a photographic supplier. However, if there is a significant quantity of dust then it is better to remove it with a vacuum cleaner because blowing the dust away will push it into the air only for it to settle elsewhere. In the long term, daily cleaning of surfaces and a periodic deep clean of equipment are necessary elements of the imaging operation and should be incorporated into the scanning schedule.

Workflow and document tracking

In this context, workflow refers to the sequence of physical processes that the documents will go through during the image capture operation. The simplest workflow for an imaging operation is for an operator to image one item at a time in numerical sequence starting with number one. However, projects will often have more complex requirements that may involve document preparation, conservation work and processing of many thousands of documents over a time span of several years. A further complication is that an imaging operation will have an impact on other users of the documents and so an efficient, robust workflow will not only benefit the imaging operation and the project as a whole but will minimize the impact on the institution.

Workflow should aim to keep the transport and handling of the original documents to a minimum. For a large-scale imaging project the requirements of the imaging system will have an influence because factors such as the speed of image capture and capacity of digital storage will determine the quantity of documents in a batch and the rate at which documents can be processed. If conservation work is incorporated into the workflow then estimates of the time needed to carry out the work must be taken into account. This means that a degree of flexibility is needed because there may be documents that need more extensive preparation by a conservator. There are several different ways in which conservation work can support an imaging operation; see Chapter 8 'Preparation of damaged documents'.

A tracking system is needed so that the location of each document and its progress in the operation is always documented. This is essential for projects where items go through several processes involving different teams, particularly since some of those teams may be physically separate, for example the conservator may be based in the conservation studio rather than the imaging area. The tracking system can also serve to alert other users when items are unavailable, and provide an estimated date of when they will become available again. For projects that involve the digitization of a collection for which there is high demand, it might be necessary to amend the catalogue to warn readers that items may not be available. It might not be feasible to withdraw an entire collection from circulation while it is being digitized so an acceptable solution would be to digitize in phased batches. If the imaging schedule is publicized then readers can look up the dates that the batches are due for digitization and see if the items they are interested in are likely to be affected.

For the purposes of the image capture operation, a tracking system can be as simple as a spreadsheet that is updated each time a document is moved, but for more complex projects a bespoke system may be developed. For example, the project to digitize part of the John Johnson collection at the Bodleian Library at Oxford involved digitization at an off-site facility. A bespoke web-based system was developed to track all individual items. This enabled items to be retrieved if requested by a researcher. The system was linked to catalogue metadata and was further developed to incorporate conservation documentation so that conservation staff could alert the imaging team if there were special requirements (Lockyer, 2009).

Staffing

Safe document handling is largely down to skills and experience; however, these are only a couple of several factors to be considered when selecting imaging staff, who will also need to be adept at operating the equipment and imaging software. Different projects will have different requirements. If a project employs a standalone scanner with simple controls then an operator with no previous experience may cope with initial training followed by *ad hoc* support. At the other extreme, for a project involving a sophisticated set-up a professional photographer might be needed, particularly if the documents themselves are challenging; for example, when imaging gold leaf decoration on a manuscript. In either case, preservation training is needed to address handling issues, as discussed below.

Good document handling comes from an understanding of the underlying preservation issues and an appreciation of the importance of preservation, and so previous experience of handling original documents or working in a library or archive context will be an advantage. For this reason in-house staff may be the best choice for a project that is particularly challenging, for example if the documents are in very poor condition. In-house staff will have experience of working with original items from the institution's collection. This means that staff have knowledge of the kinds of issues that they may encounter, can anticipate them and are capable of identifying issues and dealing with them when they arise. This could be a case of knowing when it is appropriate to seek assistance from other staff and exactly which staff to contact if they have problems.

If an institution contracts a supplier to carry out the image capture then they will have limited control over who is employed on the imaging team, even more so if the supplier then contracts a third party such as an employment agency to supply the staff. In this situation it is important to maintain a good working relationship with the supplier so that requirements are understood by both sides (see Chapter 2 'Before you digitize: resources, suppliers and surrogates'). This is not a matter of the institution imposing restrictions on the supplier – good handling is not only good for the documents but can be more efficient and reduces the need for calling out a conservator. In the long term this benefits the imaging operation and the project overall.

Very large digitization projects may have teams of project staff on short-term contracts. Projects that run for several years may have more than one complete turnaround of staff. New staff will require security clearance and training so a high turnover is undesirable simply due to the resources needed for recruitment and induction. However, retaining good staff is important for document welfare too because as an operator gains experience they will develop confidence in handling items and be able to work more efficiently as a result, while maintaining document welfare. A physically comfortable working environment, incentives and strong team leadership will all help to maintain a positive working atmosphere and hence to encourage staff retention.

For very large projects it may be appropriate to employ staff in different teams to work on different tasks. The advantage of this approach is that staff become specialized and quickly gain knowledge and experience in particular areas. The disadvantage is the lack of flexibility in the workforce when needing to cover for leave or sickness. If the work pattern will involve working in shifts then it is worth considering whether particular tasks are suited to particular shifts. For example, work that may involve liaising with conservation staff may be better suited to office hours, while tasks such as equipment calibration or maintenance may be best done late at night.

Preservation training

All project staff should receive preservation training at the outset. For in-house staff this may consist of a briefing on the particular project and its context and a run-through of particular requirements in terms of document preparation and handling. When training external contractors part of the aim should be to instil a preservation ethos so that staff understand that preservation is an important function of the institution and they can see their own role in the preservation of the collection. This has many aspects, from the way they handle documents to their wider role in the digitization of the collection. The training should also cover basic handling guidance, including restrictions such as no food and drink, as well as instruction in the processes themselves.

It is particularly important that project staff should know who to contact if they have queries or problems with a document. Training should therefore also cover types of damage likely to be encountered so that staff are confident that they know how to deal with it and when to contact a conservator. Projects can vary widely in the nature of the documents and in the equipment used so generic training may not be sufficiently detailed. If necessary, training should be adapted for each project so as to cover specific aspects of unpacking, preparing and processing the documents. One hour should be sufficient to cover an introduction to the work and demonstration of the processes.

Ongoing conservation support

An imaging operation will require ongoing support from conservation staff. A member of staff should be available to respond to queries and problems as they arise. Since such operations often run to tight deadlines it may be necessary for queries to be dealt with immediately. Often this will involve a conservator assisting or advising an operator with an issue that can be resolved on the spot. If an item needs to be taken away for conservation work then this should be carried out as soon as possible so as to minimize the impact on the workflow.

At the beginning of a project it is useful for conservation staff to carry out a follow-up session shortly after the initial preservation training. This is because processes that were developed in the planning stage may not work so well in practice and the conservator can advise on adaptations. At a later date it may be useful to carry out refresher training for the project team. This can also be a good opportunity for staff to provide feedback on handling issues they have come across.

Chapter summary

- A large-scale digitization project needs a well designed workspace in order to operate efficiently. The layout should reflect the sequence of the operation. This may mean that there are separate areas for preparation, conservation and imaging.
- The work surfaces must be large enough to enable safe document handling. Documents should always be fully supported and should never be placed on a chair or on the floor.
- The working environment should have similar restrictions to those in a reading room. The collection manager should advise on the use of tools and materials such as marker sheets.
- A system for document tracking is essential but need not be highly complex. For a very large project a tracking system can be designed with bespoke functionality.
- Good document handling comes with experience so a high staff turnover is undesirable. An institution may not have any influence over the recruitment of imaging staff but all project staff should receive preservation training.

Bibliography

Frey, F. S. and Reilly, J. M. (2006) *Digital Imaging for Photographic Collections: foundations for technical standards,* 2nd edn, Image Permanence Institute, www.imagepermanenceinstitute.org/shtml_sub/digibook.pdf.

Library of Congress (1999) *Conservation Implications of Digitization Projects,* National Digital Library Program and the Conservation Division, http://lcweb2.loc.gov/ammem/techdocs/conserv83199a.pdf.

Lockyer, L. (2009) Capturing a collection, *ICON News: the magazine of the Institute of Conservation,* **21** (March), 18–21.

Palm, J. (2010) personal communication.

Conclusion

Digitizing collections means much more than taking images. Common perceptions of digitization projects requiring a scanner, a scanning operator and an item to be scanned, do not do justice to the often highly complex process of planning and preparing for digitization, image capture, quality control and metadata creation, eventually leading to successful online delivery of content. For an institution to own a set of digital images does not automatically mean that its collections are any more accessible than they were prior to digitization.

Digitization may have two functions within the context of managing collections: digital surrogates may serve as access copies instead of the originals, therefore aiding its preservation through less handling requirements; or they may be used to reach new audiences through online delivery. In both cases, the aims can only be fulfilled if image quality is optimal for the intended purpose, taking into account current and future audiences, and planning for the future preservation of both the original collections as well as the digital surrogate. Making information accessible through online channels also requires appropriate finding systems, such as a catalogue, to be in place, as well as a retrieval system in order to deliver content to the user.

The collection manager, with their eye for detail as well as their knowledge of materials and formats, will have a lot to contribute to the successful implementation of digitization projects. Supporting the digitization of collections does not just mean facilitating the image capture process by providing the documents; it is not a matter of following the same well known protocols time and again for every project. Rather, it is about gathering knowledge about individual collections and their users, and using this knowledge to inform all practical aspects of such ventures, including resource requirements, workflow and equipment. Their involvement will ensure that image quality is as good as it can get; but they will also enable cost-effective running of such projects by making sure that potential problems during scanning have been dealt with before they arise.

Digitization undoubtedly has an impact on an institution's conservation studio, and conservators will need to adapt their work in the digitization context. However, the conservator's skill set is entirely compatible with the digitization of heritage collections. Where digitization aims to preserve and use the collection, a conservator is well placed to make judgements on balancing preservation and use. This will typically mean respect for the original material through minimum intervention in order to retain as much original value as possible. Digitization does not require robust treatments, but rather stabilizing items to a degree that allows them to withstand the imaging process: as much as necessary, as little as possible. In addition, preparing historic collections for digitization requires a pragmatic approach, enabling the process through minimizing risks.

At the same time, a successful digitization project will have to include all relevant stakeholders from the very beginning. Curators, repository staff, copyright lawyers, scanning companies and operators, marketing and public services professionals and digital preservation professionals all have vital roles to play. Their combined contributions from the start will ensure that the resulting product, whether intended for preservation or online presentation, is fit for purpose at the end. This also implies that digitization projects have to be very carefully planned in order to ensure that all requirements and opinions have been considered. Rectification of problems occurring during image capture will be much more time-consuming, and therefore costly, than planning ahead, anticipating potential pitfalls and mitigating them before the start of the project.

The key, then, to successful digitization is collaboration, planning, preparation and presentation.

Further reading

General guidelines

Federal Agencies Digitization Guidelines Initiative: Still Image Working Group (2009) *Documents and Guidelines*, www.digitizationguidelines.gov/stillimages/documents.html.
A group of US federal agencies including the Library of Congress, the National Archives and Records Administration, and the Smithsonian Institution, began meeting in 2007 with the aim to develop common digitization guidelines. The Still Image Working Group has released numerous draft documents and guidelines online including a digital conversion bibliography. The initiative is ongoing and welcomes feedback from users.

Federal Agencies Digitization Guidelines Initiative: Still Image Working Group: Digitization Standards (2010) *Technical Guidelines for Digitizing Cultural Heritage Materials: Creation of Raster Image Master Files*, www.digitizationguidelines.gov/stillimages/documents/ FADGITechnicalGuidelines-2010-06.pdf.
This publication from the Still Image Working Group covers technical and practical aspects of digitization.

Hughes, L. (2004) *Digitizing Collections: strategic issues for the information manager*, Facet Publishing.
Digitizing Collections covers strategic issues in detail including funding and project management. It includes digitization of audio and moving image collections.

Sitts, M. (ed.) (2000) *Handbook for Digital Projects: a management tool for preservation and access: first edition*, Northeast Document Conservation Centre, www.nedcc.org/resources/digitalhandbook/dighome.htm.

Published by the Northeast Document Conservation Centre in the USA this provides detailed advice from a range of practitioners from different institutions, and includes a number of case studies. Much of the advice is applicable to museums as well as libraries and archives.

UNESCO (2002) *Guidelines for Digitization Projects: for collections and holdings in the public domain, particularly those held by libraries and archives,* http://portal.unesco.org/en/ev.php-URL_ID=7315&URL_DO=DO_TOPIC&URL_SECTION=201.html.

These guidelines were drawn up by IFLA (International Federation of Library Associations) and ICA (International Council of Archives) on behalf of UNESCO (United Nations Educational, Scientific and Cultural Organization). Gives an overview of all main issues. Each section has a bibliography.

The digital image

Federal Agencies Digitization Guidelines Initiative: Still Image Working Group: Digitization Standards (2010) *A Resource List for Standards Related to Digital Imaging of Print, Graphic, and Pictorial Materials,* www.digitizationguidelines.gov/stillimages/digstandards.html.

This annotated list provides an overview of standards and best practices concerning digitization and digital storage.

Frey, F. S. and Reilly, J. M. (2006) *Digital Imaging for Photographic Collections: foundations for technical standards: second edition,* Image Permanence Institute, www.imagepermanenceinstitute.org/shtml_sub/digibook.pdf.

First published in 1999 this publication resulted from a two year research project to study digital imaging in libraries and archives. It provides a framework for image standards with a focus on digitization of photographic collections, although it does not specify an image specification standard.

Public Record Office Victoria (2010) *Digitisation: image requirements,* www.prov.vic.gov.au/publications/publns/1002s2.pdf.

This image capture standard was published by the Public Record Office Victoria with the intention of establishing the minimum technical requirements for the digitization of government records in the State of Victoria, Australia. It applies when digitizing with a view to replace paper records with digital copies and provides specifications for a range of different source materials.

Equipment for image capture

JISC Digital Media (2009) *Digital Cameras*,
www.jiscdigitalmedia.ac.uk/stillimages/advice/digital-cameras.
JISC Digital Media (2009) *Scanners*,
www.jiscdigitalmedia.ac.uk/stillimages/advice/scanners.
JISC Digital Media is a service which aims to enhance digital media resources for
Further and Higher Education in the UK by providing advice and guidance.
Their online advice includes numerous articles offering useful introductions to a
range of subjects, including digital cameras and scanners. JISC Digital Media is
supported by JISC (Joint Information Systems Committee).
Williams, D. (2000) Selecting a Scanner. In Colet, L. S., D'Amato, D., Frey, F. and
Williams, D., *Guides to Quality in Visual Resource Imaging*, DLF (Digital Library
Federation), CLIR (Council on Library and Information Resources) and RLG
(Research Libraries Group),
www.diglib.org/pubs/dlf091.
One of five guides commissioned by the Digital Library Federation and the
Council on Library and Information Resources, and published online by the
Research Libraries Group. This guide focuses on technical aspects of choosing
equipment for image capture including how to interpret and compare product
specifications and how to evaluate the resulting digital images.

Index